Signless

Buddha-Mindfulness

Also by Venerable Xiao Pingshi

The Correct Meanings of the Āgamas: Exploring the Origin of the Consciousness-Only Doctrine (7 vol.)
《阿含正義—唯識學探源》

An Exposition on the Laṅkāvatāra Sūtra (10 vol.)
《楞伽經詳解》

A Discourse on the Śūraṅgama Sūtra (15 vol.)
《楞嚴經講記》

A Discourse on the Vimalakīrti Sūtra (6 vol.)
《維摩詰經講記》

Mastering the Essence of the Diamond Sūtra (9 vol.)
《金剛經宗通》

The Secret Meanings of the Heart Sūtra
《心經密意》

Perfect Harmony between Chan and Pure Land
《禪淨圓融》

Chan: Before and After Enlightenment
《禪—悟前與悟後》

The True versus the False Enlightenment
《真假開悟》

The Undeniable Existence of the Tathāgatagarbha
《真實如來藏》

Mastering and Skillfully Articulating the Essence of Buddhist Enlightenment: The Way to Buddhahood
《宗通與說通—成佛之道》

Wrong Views versus the Buddha Dharma
《邪見與佛法》

The Seventh and Eighth Mental Consciousnesses?
The Supra-Consciousness that Transcends Time and Space
《第七意識與第八意識？—穿越時空「超意識」》

Behind the Façade of Secret Mantra (4 vol.)
《狂密與真密》

Signless

Buddha-Mindfulness

The Principle and Entrance Expedients of
Bodhisattva Mahāsthāmaprāpta's Dharma-Door
for Perfect Mastery through Buddha-Mindfulness

Xiao Pingshi

Wholesome Vision ™

About the Author

Born in 1944, Venerable Master Xiao Pingshi (蕭平實) was raised in a farming family in central Taiwan. Seeking answers to the truth of human existence, he became a committed Buddhist disciple and practitioner in his forties and in 1990, attained awakening to the True Mind via Chan contemplation and the aid of an incredible Dharma-door called "signless Buddha-mindfulness."

In 1997, Master Xiao established the Buddhist True Enlightenment Practitioners Association in order to offer different levels of Dharma classes to practitioners. Presently, the Association's practice centers have reached all major cities of Taiwan, and beyond to Hong Kong and the United States. Since the founding of the Association, Master Xiao has been giving weekly lecture on important Buddhist scriptures, such as the *Laṅkāvatāra Sūtra,* the *Śūraṅgama Sūtra*, the *Sūtra on Upāsaka Precepts*, the *Śrīmālādevī Siṃhanāda Sūtra,* the *Diamond Sūtra*, the *Lotus Sūtra*, and so forth.

To elucidate the Buddha Dharma and its stages of cultivation for all interested learners, Master Xiao has also published more than a hundred books on a wide range of Buddhist subjects. These include the combined cultivation of Chan and Pure Land, the realization of the Path to Liberation expounded in the Āgamas, the analysis of the profound Middle-Way teachings and the exegesis of key Consciousness-Only scriptures. All of his books emphasize the points that Buddhism is a path of personal realization and that realization can only come through a continual process of listening to, contemplating, and actual practice of the Buddha Dharma.

Contents

Translator's Note

The practice of Buddha-mindfulness introduced in this book is deliberately coined "signless Buddha-mindfulness" for reasons worthy of discussion and clarification so that readers can better appreciate this convenient yet incredibly efficacious method. In Buddhist literature, the word *sign* is a common translation of the Sanskrit word *nimitta*, which denotes the distinguishing characteristics of everything within the three realms of existence in Buddhist cosmology. For instance, in the Pure Land practice of Buddha-mindfulness, the Buddha's name or image visualized are both a kind of sign or attribute that help keeps one's attention on a particular Buddha.

First and foremost, this practice of Buddha-mindfulness is characterized as "signless" to highlight the fact that it is an expedient that could bring about the direct realization of the signless True Mind, the origin of all phenomenal existence that Buddhist practitioners seek enlightenment to. Technically speaking, the wordless and formless awareness and recollection of Buddha in "signless Buddha-mindfulness" is still a representation and, therefore, a sign, albeit a much subtler one compared to the readily perceivable and comprehensible signs like Buddha's sacred name, physical appearance, or virtuous deeds. Nevertheless, by virtue of being a very subtle representation of Buddha, this wordless and formless bare thought can effectively facilitate the direct perception of the True Mind, the mind entity free of any signs associated with the three realms and known as the self-nature, the intrinsic Buddha, the True Suchness, the Dharma-body of Buddha, the eighth consciousness, the *ālayavijñāna*, the *tathāgatagarbha* in Buddhist scriptures. When a practitioner has attained direct and personal realization of the True Mind the Buddha-mindfulness he or she practices is essentially the "signless mindfulness" in its purest sense.

Secondly, this practice of Buddha-mindfulness is named "signless" to set it apart from the common methods of Buddha-mindfulness such as name recitation and visualization, which sustain mental focus through "signs" like words, sounds, images associated with the Buddha, or even the concepts of Buddha's sublime attributes and virtues. As the author points out and explains in this book, the cultivation of Buddha-mindfulness should begin with the use of coarser forms and signs to help restrain a scattered mind from restlessness and mental disturbances. However, when a practitioner's mind becomes more unified and focused, he or she must switch to a subtler sign at appropriate junctures to train the mind to reach an even higher degree of mental absorption.

By following the methods and cultivation sequence detailed in this book, a practitioner will not only improve his or her level of mental concentration and achieve a mind of one-pointedness but also be able to hold a bare thought of Buddha in mind regardless whether he or she is in stillness or in physical motion. For a Pure Land practitioners, this level of proficiency in meditative absorption reduces their reliance on signs and forms during practice and propels them closer to the goal of gaining rebirth in Buddha's pure land at the end of this current lifetime. For Chan practitioners, the ability to maintain one-pointed absorption in physical motion enables them to competently contemplate *huatou* or *gong'an*, so that eventually they could break through the "sense of doubt" and attain sudden awakening to the True Mind. This skillful application of Buddha-mindfulness as an effective means to enhance meditative concentration and facilitate Chan awakening aptly illustrates the dual cultivation of the Chan and Pure Land traditions as well as their complementary nature.

Preface

For most Buddhist learners, the term "Buddha-mindfulness" (念佛) simply means the recitation of the sacred name of a particular Buddha or bodhisattva. With utmost faith as well as pious and continuous recitation, practitioners take refuge in Buddhas and bodhisattvas and hope to obtain connection with them either through subtle responses or visual manifestations. The most common reason for practicing Buddha-mindfulness is to be guided by Buddha (Amitābha) and bodhisattvas to take rebirth in the Pure Land of Ultimate Bliss at the end of the current life. However, Buddha Amitābha's Pure Land of Ultimate Bliss is far from being *the* only pure land. There are actually countless pure lands manifested by Buddhas in the worlds of ten directions, including that of our Fundamental Teacher—Buddha Śākyamuni. A distinction should also be made between the Mind-Only Pure Land (唯心淨土) and pure lands manifested by various Buddhas.

In a broad sense, all cultivation methods of Mahāyāna Buddhism fall within the scope of the Pure Land school's Dharma-door of Buddha-mindfulness, including well-known practices such as recitation of Buddha's name, mantra chanting, prostration, offering making, tranquility and insight meditation (*śamathavipaśyanā*), observance of precepts, as well as the chanting, copying, studying, expounding, reflecting on, contemplating of sūtras, and so forth. They are all geared toward learning the practices of Buddha, understanding the Dharma, attaining liberation, acquiring the meritorious qualities of Buddha, and ultimately, realizing the four types of pure land upon the attainment of Buddhahood.

The Pure Land tradition is inseparably intertwined with the Chan school. To attain Buddhahood, a Buddhist practitioner cannot simply recite Buddha's name but has to draw upon the power of meditative concentration (*samādhi*) to directly and personally realize the True Mind. Having realized the True Mind, a practitioner gains vision of the bodhisattva path and can swiftly advance to the stage of cultivation, which means bringing within sight the eventual attainment of Buddhahood. In order to "see the path," however, he must utilize either Chan contemplation or the method of "contemplation of the principle (理觀)" in the cultivation of tranquility and insight meditation to realize the True Mind. Both of these methods call for a sufficient degree of meditative concentration, especially the ability to maintain meditative concentration while one is in physical motion.

In fact, the power of meditative concentration is essential to Pure Land practitioners if they are to achieve one-pointed absorption through the recitation of Buddha's name. If recitation of Buddha's name and prostration to Buddha are used together as expedient techniques to build up the power of meditative concentration, it is actually not difficult for Pure Land practitioners to enter Bodhisattva Mahāsthāmaprāpta's Dharma-door for perfect mastery through Buddha-mindfulness, an accomplishment that will help secure rebirth in the Pure Land of Ultimate Bliss. Alternatively, once they have acquired a decent level of meditative concentration, a Pure Land practitioner may also choose to proceed to the practice of contemplative Buddha-mindfulness, through which they could "spontaneously awaken to the True Mind without employing skillful means." If, instead, they apply the power of meditative concentration gained from the entry practice of Bodhisattva Mahāsthāmaprāpta's Dharma-door of Buddha-mindfulness toward Chan contemplation, they could also awaken to the True Mind as the "gateless gate" will reveal itself spontaneously. One can see that the cultivation methods of Chan and Pure Land are clearly inseparable from one another.

If a Buddhist disciple cultivates the Dharma-door of the Pure Land following the essentials of samādhi cultivation and use the Pure Land methods to enhance his power of in-motion meditative concentration, he can make quick and equal progress in both Chan and Pure Land practices. I humbly put forth the above views for the sole purpose of benefiting all readers and set aside concerns for my own reputation as I put thought to paper.

I would like to give a brief account of the events that led up to this book. At the beginning of 1987, my hectic work schedule allowed me no time for meditation at all. Every evening I was extremely weary during my recitation of the *Diamond Sūtra* and I usually concluded this daily routine with prostrations to the Buddha immediately right after.

One summer evening that year, as I was prostrating to the Buddha, it suddenly dawned on me that I should drop the name and image of Buddha and instead only keep a pure thought of Buddha during prostration. I tried out my intuition right away. From the next day on, I started to make prostrations while bearing only a thought of Buddha in mind, a method I have since termed "signless Buddha-mindfulness." As time went by, I became proficient in signless mindfulness through consistent practice. I was filled with Dharma-joy and was impermeable to stress and fatigue of worldly living. Deriving so much joy from this practice, I even ceased my old evening routine and concentrated on the practice of prostration with signless mindfulness of Buddha. During the rest of the day, I held a signless pure thought of Buddha in mind amidst my daily activities.

By the end of 1988, the thought of sharing my Dharma-joy with fellow practitioners crossed my mind. I started to sift through my memory and jotted down each and every step I took to accomplish my practice. At the same time, I scoured and reviewed sūtras and treatises to locate scriptural verification of my method. Right before completing the draft to this book, I came upon the section "Bodhisattva Mahāsthāmaprāpta's Dharma-door for Perfect Mastery through Buddha-Mindfulness (大勢至菩薩念佛圓通章)" in the *Śūraṅgama Sūtra*. I was elated when my eyes set upon the words "recollect and be mindful of Buddha." As I read on and saw, "rein in all six sense faculties and abide in one continuous pure thought to enter samādhi," I realized that my method was precisely the Dharma-door of perfect mastery through Buddha-mindfulness illustrated by Bodhisattva Mahāsthāmaprāpta.

Subsequently in April 1989, I compiled my notes into a short essay entitled "A Discussion of Signless Buddha-Prostration and Buddha-Mindfulness." After I finished the draft of this article, I came upon the writings of Venerable Xuyun (虛 雲 和 尚) and finally acquired a clear understanding of the principle and method regarding the guarding of a *huatou* (話頭).[1] Only then did I realize that, while I thought I was contemplating *huatou* and boldly claimed I was doing so, all along I was merely uttering words and observing its trail.

Why was I not able to contemplate *huatou* in my earlier attempts? It was simple: at the beginning I didn't have the ability to maintain a focused mind in motion. Only after I mastered the signless mindfulness of Buddha was I able to maintain a focused mind in motion and hence contemplate *huatou*.

In the afternoon of August 6, 1989, I twice entered into a state of "seeing the mountain as not being mountain" during a group practice and experienced for the first time the state of a "dark barrel." After that, I wavered in and out of a mass of doubt. In early November of 1989, after I came back from a pilgrimage to India and Nepal, I decided to close my business to focus on Chan contemplation at home. On the second day of the eleventh lunar month in 1990, my Chan contemplation lasted until around four o' clock in the afternoon when the "dark barrel" was eventually smashed.

In retrospect, I realized that the root cause for most practitioners' lack of progress in their Dharma practice is the inability to maintain meditative concentration in

---

[1] *Huatou* 話頭: literally "word head," *huatou* refers to what comes before words. It should be noted that while *hua* means spoken words in Chinese, in the Chan context it should be understood as a thought or idea associated with linguistic contents or images. *Huatou*, therefore, refers to the wordless and imageless awareness prior to such a thought is formed in mind. In the Chan school, the guarding and contemplation of *huatou* is a pedagogical device used to help practitioners uncover the True Mind.

motion. This book was written to help practitioners swiftly attain an undisturbed mind during their practice of Buddha-mindfulness, a skill with which they can quickly move on to the contemplation of *huatou* and *gong'an* (公案).[2]

At the request of fellow practitioners, I gave a weekly lecture on signless Buddha-mindfulness (i.e. the expedient way of entering Bodhisattva Mahāsthāmaprāpta's Dharma-door for perfect mastery through Buddha-mindfulness) for three consecutive weeks starting from September 3, 1991. These three lectures were held at the Chan center of a Buddhist society of a financial institution and at Mr. and Mrs. Chen's residence in Shipai, all in Taipei.

There were altogether thirty people at the time in these two practice groups. Most of them used recitation of Buddha's name as their practice method. By putting what they learned from my lectures into actual practice, two of them were able to accomplish signless Buddha-mindfulness within merely six weeks. After three months, six people had mastered this practice. As of today (February 28, 1992), thirteen people have mastered it in a time span of less than six months. Still more people are joining in and making speedy progress. The rate of mastery and the speed of progress are very encouraging. Excluding those who did not practice prostration due to individual conditions, the main reason for the others' lack of progress was their aversion to

---

[2] *Gong'an* 公案: this term, known as "*koan*" in Japanese, carries the literal meaning of "public case" or "precedent." A *gong'an* in the Chan tradition typically consists of dialogues between a Chan master and his disciple(s). Like *huatou*, a Chan practitioner is supposed to contemplate the meaning of *gong'an* without using any language or image in order to achieve sudden awakening to the True Mind.

this method and its preparatory expedients, that is, the recitation of Buddha's name. When they finally changed their minds after seeing that those who had mastered this method were starting to guard *huatou* and contemplate Chan, they were already three to four months behind.

These results and observations excited me greatly. They showed that signless mindfulness of Buddha could definitely be mastered when it is facilitated by expedient methods and practiced with continuous diligence. Out of my deep dismay at the decline of the Buddha Dharma and the desire to free sentient beings from their sufferings, I committed myself to another compassionate vow and put together this book with great haste during the winter break. My writing is far from elegant but I try to articulate myself clearly and coherently. For easy comprehension, I wrote in a colloquial style as much as possible and narrated in a plain, direct, and somewhat repetitive manner to get my points across. May all Buddhist practitioners master signless Buddha-mindfulness, be filled with Dharma-joy, spread this method to benefit countless beings, and enter the Ocean of the Vairocana Nature.

Take refuge in our Fundamental Teacher Buddha Śākyamuni
Take refuge in Bodhisattva Avalokiteśvara of Great Compassion
Take refuge in Bodhisattva Mahāsthāmaprāpta

A disciple of the Three Jewels
Xiao Pingshi
Feb 28, 1992

Chapter 1

Introduction

Bodhisattva Mahāsthāmaprāpta's Dharma-door for perfect mastery through Buddha-Mindfulness is taken from the section "Bodhisattva Mahāsthāmaprāpta's Dharma-door for Perfect Mastery through Buddha-Mindfulness" in Vol. 5 of *The Great Śūraṅgama Sūtra on Hidden Basis of the Tathāgata's Myriad Bodhisattva Practices Leading to The Verification of the Ultimate Truth Spoken from the Crown of the Buddha's Head.* This sūtra, commonly referred to in short as the *Śūraṅgama Sūtra* (楞嚴經), is a required reading for practitioners of both meditative concentration (*samādhi*) and Chan contemplation. It contains the accounts of twenty-five bodhisattvas explaining their respective cultivation methods, followed by Bodhisattva Mañjuśrī's comment that the Dharma-door for perfect mastery through the ear faculty (耳根圓通法門) illustrated by Bodhisattva Avalokiteśvara is the most fitting for sentient beings in this world.

As of today, the time of the saints is far behind us and our lifestyle has become bustling and busy; the relaxing rustic lifestyle of the countryside is impractical for most. A modern person can at best spare one or two hours a day to practice the Dharma-door for the mastery through the ear faculty. Unless he is very skilled in meditation and has come up with some useful and practical ways to aid his practice, it is not at all easy to succeed in this specific Dharma-door.

According to the *Śūraṅgama Sūtra*, Bodhisattva Mahāsthāmaprāpta's Dharma-door for perfect mastery through Buddha-mindfulness is regarded as the second best to Bodhisattva Avalokiteśvara's Dharma-door for perfect mastery through the ear faculty. In my opinion, Bodhisattva Mahāsthāmaprāpta's method is the most compatible with today's hurried lifestyle. And unsurprisingly, this Dharma-door of Buddha-mindfulness has been recommended and advocated by many prominent contemporary Buddhist figures in writing or through other media.

Chan is the objective of personal realization in my Dharma cultivation. However, in my early years of cultivation, I spent considerable amount of time trying to practice Chan contemplation but to no avail. My mind was terribly distracted because of my demanding schedule. Although I set aside time for sitting meditation every day, I never had more than an hour for it. All that I gained was the ability to maintain a focused mind in stillness. As soon as I rose from the meditation cushion, my focused mind gave way to restlessness. I did not have the slightest idea what Chan was really about, let alone the ability to contemplate it. It was not until I mastered the signless Buddha-mindfulness at the end of 1988 did I finally uncover the "gateless gate" of the Chan school. In May 1989, I drew upon my skill of singless Buddha-mindfulness to contemplate Chan. I strove and persisted for eighteen grueling months, during which I enjoyed neither sleep nor food, before finally breaking through the gateless gate.

Through this experience, I realized that most people in our modern world find the contemplation of Chan so challenging is primarily because of inadequate power of meditative concentration, specifically, the ability to maintain meditative concentration in motion, which is a prerequisite for Chan contemplation. Let's use the Chan practice of *huatou* as an example to illustrate this. A *huatou* is defined by the Venerable Xuyun in the following way:

> What is a *huatou*? *Hua* means words and *tou* means the moment before words are spoken. For example, the utterance "Amitābha" is a *hua*, while *huatou* is the moment before these words are formed in the mind. Therefore, *huatou* is the moment before a single thought has arisen. Once a thought has arisen, it is already the tail end of *hua*. The moment before a thought is called "non-arising"; not losing this moment, not letting your mind go dull, not attached to quiescence, and not falling into nothingness is called "non-ceasing." The moment to moment, continuous, and single-minded reflexive illumination of this "neither arising nor ceasing" is called guarding a *huatou*, or tending a *huatou*.[3]

In other words, in order to guard a *huatou*, one must be able to abide in the moment before a thought emerges; or put another way, one must have the ability to remain attentive to the moment before the chosen thought arises in mind. This is the correct way to guard a *huatou*. On the

---

[3] Xuyun 虛雲, *Xuyun laoheshang fangbian kaishi lu* 虛雲老和尚方便開示錄 [Taiwan (Nantou): Chung Tai Shan Buddhist Foundation, 1997.], p. 52: 什麼叫做話頭？話就是説話，頭就是説話之前。如念「阿彌陀佛」是句話, 未念之前就是話頭。所謂話頭就是一念未生之際。一念才生，已是話尾。這一念未生之際叫做不生，不掉舉，不昏沉，不著靜，不落空，叫做不滅。時時刻刻，單單的的一念，迴光返照。這不生不滅就叫做看話頭，或照顧話頭。

contrary, one would be watching the trail of a thought (*huawei*) if one recites a *huatou* like "Who is bearing the Buddha in mind?" orally or silently in mind, or if one ponders over the answer to this interrogative. This is because in all these cases, one is already at the end of the words or the thought of "Who is bearing the Buddha in mind?" Hence Venerable Xuyun states:

> Why, in this modern age, do many practice the guarding of *huatou* but few achieve awakening? One explanation is that the capacity of modern men is inferior to that of their ancient predecessors. Another problem is that most learners have never understood the principle of Chan contemplation and the correct way to guard a *huatou*. Some have traveled all over, searching far and wide, without ever figuring out what a *huatou* really is and how to guard it. They cling to language and terms all their lives, occupying themselves with the *huawei*.[4]

If a practitioner is capable of guarding a *huatou*, he will be able to contemplate Chan. If not, he must make it a priority to strengthen his power of in-motion concentration in order to acquire the ability to guard a *huatou* amidst all daily activities. Then, he can move on to Chan contemplation and speed up his Dharma cultivation.

Gong'an and *huatou* are two variations of the same

---

[4] Ibid., pp. 41-42: 然而為什麼現代的人，看話頭的多，而悟道的人沒有幾個呢？這個由於現代的人，根器不及古人。亦由學者對於參禪看話頭的理路，多是沒有摸清。有的人東參西訪，南奔北走，結果鬧到老，對一個話頭還沒有弄明白，不知什麼是話頭，如何才算看話頭？一生總是執著言句名相，在話尾上用心。

thing and the contemplation of both is predicated on the ability to keep the mind in one-pointed focus without any discursive thoughts arising. For this reason, Venerable Xuyun says:

> Among all the sayings of Patriarch Bodhidharma and the Sixth Patriarch, the most significant is "suspend one's attention to all external states and abide in a mind without any distracting thoughts." To "suspend one's attention to all external states" means to let go of all external things. Together, these two statements "let go of all external states" and "abide in a mind without any distracting thoughts" highlight the prerequisite skill for Chan contemplation. If one cannot let go and abide as stated, not only will one not succeed in Chan contemplation, it is not even possible for one to get a foot in the door of Chan...[5]

He also says:

> Before the Tang and Song dynasties, most Chan masters attained awakening to the path upon hearing a word or phrase, and the transmission between master and disciples was merely through "verifying the mind with the mind"; there was no formal method to go about it. The daily exchanges between master and disciples were merely for the untying of entanglements, in the way medicines are prescribed according to

---

[5] Ibid., p. 38: 達摩祖師和六祖開示學人最要緊的話，莫若「屏息諸緣，一念不生」。屏息諸緣就是萬緣放下，所以「萬緣放下，一念不生」這兩句話，實在是參禪的先決條件。這兩句話如果做不到，參禪不但是說沒有成功，就是入門都不可能...。

the ills. After the Song Dynasty, people's potential were not as good as their predecessors and they could no longer put what they were taught into practice. For example, while practitioners were taught to "let go of all" and "not thinking neither good nor ill," they could not let go and kept putting their thoughts to either good or ill nonetheless. In view of this, the patriarchs had no choice but to make learners contemplate *gong'an* as a way of purging poison with poison.[6]

And:

The ancients had many *gong'ans*, but later on the emphasis was shifted to the guarding of *huatou*....The two are actually the same....*Hua* [words] arises from the mind, thus the mind is the *tou* [the moment prior to the arising] of *hua*. Thoughts likewise emerge from the mind, thus the mind is what precedes thoughts. All dharmas originate from the mind, thus the mind is what comes before all dharmas. In fact, *huatou* is the moment prior to the arising of a thought, and the moment prior to the arising of a thought is the mind. To put it more directly, *huatou* is the state of mind before a thought has arisen.[7]

---

[6] Ibid., p. 40: 在唐宋以前的禪德，多是由一言半句就悟道了。師徒間的傳授，不過以心印心，並沒有什麼實法。平日參問酬答，也不過隨方解縛，因病與藥而已。宋代以後，人們的根器陋劣了，講了做不到；譬如說「放下一切」，「善惡莫作」；但總是放不下，不是思善，就是思惡。到了這個時候，祖師不得已，採取以毒攻毒的辦法，教學人參公案。

[7] Ibid., pp. 40-41: 古人的公案多得很，後來專講看話頭....其實都一

The above elaboration of Venerable Xuyun makes it clear that the contemplation of both *gong'an* and *huatou* requires the ability to maintain one's mind in a state without distracting thoughts. However, it must be pointed out that the ability to maintain such a mental state is but a description given to laymen—those who are truly in possession of this ability know very well that it actually refers to the ability "to abide continuously in one-pointed focus."

The entryway of Chan is a gateless gate. It stresses the "elimination of the path of language and the cessation of all workings of the mind." So how is it possible for one to attain awakening if every single thought of one's mind is occupied with linguistic expressions and mental analysis? Even if such a person is forced into an awakening with the help of an enlightened Chan master, most likely he will not be able to sustain his attainment and will regress from it in a matter of minutes, hours, or days. Why is that? Because he does not possess adequate power of meditative concentration—specifically, the ability to maintain a focused mind while one is in physical motion.

The ability to maintain in-motion meditative concentration is crucial for Pure Land practitioners as much as for Chan practitioners. The various Pure Land Dharma-doors commonly practiced today, such as the chanting of mantras, the recitation of Buddha's name, or the sixteen ways of visualization, all require this ability cannot be easily accomplished without the ability to sustain in-motion meditative concentration.

I have met elderly practitioners who have chanted

樣....話從心起，心是話之頭；念從心起，心是念之頭；萬法皆從心生，心是萬法之頭。其實，話頭就是念頭，念之前頭就是心。直言之，一念未生前，就是話頭。

Buddha's name for more than a decade. When asked whether they are confident about taking rebirth in the Pure Land of Ultimate Bliss, they looked nervous and didn't dare to answer. It seemed that everyone hoped to but nobody could be certain. One cannot help but wonder how many people actually have full confidence in their rebirth there. On this subject, the writings in the sūtras are clear and plain:

> If, when I attain Buddhahood, sentient beings in the ten directions who, having heard my name, entrust themselves to me with utmost faith and delight, dedicate all their virtuous roots toward rebirth in my land, and think of me just ten times, should not be born there, I will not attain perfect enlightenment. This excludes, however, those who have committed the five heinous sins and slandered the true Dharma.[8]

And:

> ... if for one day, or for two ... or up to seven days, one holds the sacred name of Buddha Amitābha with one-pointed concentration, and toward the end of his life, his mind is not confused, he will be born into the Ultimate Bliss Pure Land of Buddha Amitābha.[9]

---

[8] See *Sūtra on the Buddha of Infinite Life; Foshuo wuliangshou jing* 佛說無量壽經 (CEBTA, T12, no. 360, 268a26): 設我得佛，十方眾生至心信樂欲生我國，乃至十念，若不生者，不取正覺，唯除五逆、誹謗正法。And also the same sūtra, 268b3-5: 設我得佛，十方眾生聞我名號、係念我國，殖諸德本、至心迴向欲生我國，不果遂者，不取正覺。

[9] *Amitābha Sūtra; Foshuo amituo jing* 佛說阿彌陀經 (CEBTA, T12, no. 366, 347b9): ...若一日、若二日、若三日、若四日、若五日、若六

Given these clear instructions in the sūtras, one can examine whether during practice one can develop utmost faith and dedicate all the merits to rebirth in the pure land while maintaining ten thoughts of Buddha Amitābha in mind, or whether one is able to keep the mind in one-pointed focus totally free from distracting thoughts. If either is beyond one's ability now, how can one expect to do so toward the end of life, when one is tormented by all sorts of afflictions? Understandably, those who are aware that they cannot meet the conditions stipulated in the sūtras spend their days in endless apprehension.

This predicament haunts not only practitioners of Buddha-mindfulness but also those who practice mantra chanting or visualization. Its underlying cause is once again the insufficient power of meditative concentration.

Within the Tripiṭaka and the twelve divisions of scriptures, the Sūtra Piṭaka consists the discourses delivered by the Buddha, which focus primarily on the cultivation of meditative concentration (whereas the Vinaya Piṭaka is a collection of the Buddha's teachings regarding precepts and the Abhidharma Piṭaka the bodhisattvas' teachings on wisdom). Essentially, the "acceptance, reading, recitation, writing, and exposition of the sūtras" are all methods to train meditative concentration, a clear indication of its vital importance. A person with sufficient proficiency in meditative concentration can easily restrain the six sense faculties (*indriya*) and abide in one continuous pure thought. When one possesses this level of concentration, what worries would one still have about gaining rebirth in Buddha's pure land? But how can one develop the power of meditative

---

日、若七日，一心不亂。其人臨命終時，阿彌陀佛與諸聖眾現在其前。是人終時，心不顛倒，即得往生阿彌陀佛極樂國土。

concentration while in motion and in stillness? My experience shows that Bodhisattva Mahāsthāmaprāpta's Dharma-door for the perfect mastery through Buddha-mindfulness is the best method.

The cultivation of Buddha-mindfulness should proceed from relying on signs to disposing of them, and then to the use of signless mindfulness of Buddha as an expedient means to realize the Ultimate Reality. For this reason, practitioners of Buddha-mindfulness should be aware of the three types of Buddha-mindfulness:

1. The mindfulness of Buddha's emanation-body (*nirmāṇakāya*), as in the recitation of Buddha's name illustrated in the *Amitābha Sūtra*. The attainment of the Buddha-Mindfulness Samādhi (念 佛 三 昧) through the recitation of Buddha's name enables one to see the emanation-body (or embodiments) of Buddha Amitābha upon empathetic connections.

2. The mindfulness of Buddha's reward-body (*saṃbhogakāya*), as in the practice of the sixteen visualizations illustrated in the *Sūtra on the Contemplation of Buddha Amitāyus* (*Foshuo guan wuliangshoufo jing*; 佛說觀無量壽佛經). When the Buddha-Mindfulness Samādhi through visualization is accomplished, one can see the magnificent reward-body of Buddha Amitābha endowed with thirty-two majestic features and eighty excellent marks, or even the remarkable features of the Pure Land of Ultimate Bliss.

3. The mindfulness of Buddha's Dharma-body (*dharmakāya*), as in the signless mindfulness of Buddha via the "recollection and mindfulness of

Buddha" described in the section "Bodhisattva Mahāsthāmaprāpta's Dharma-door for Perfect Mastery through Buddha-Mindfulness" of the Śūraṅgama Sūtra. When a person has successfully mastered signless Buddha-mindfulness, he will "spontaneously awaken to the True Mind without employing any other skillful means than the recollection and mindfulness of Buddha." This person can certainly gain rebirth in the highest grade of the highest level in the Realm of True Reward and Adornment in the Pure Land of Ultimate Bliss. All he needs to do is, with utmost sincerity and the deepest faith, dedicate his merits to and make vows for rebirth in the Pure Land. As for those who have mastered signless Buddha-mindfulness but have not awakened to the True Mind, so long as they have acquired proficient understanding of the ultimate truth expounded in the Mahāyāna Vaipulya scriptures without being intimidated by it, they can be born in the Realm of True Reward and Adornment in the middle grade of the highest level if they dedicate their wholesome roots for rebirth in the Pure Land. In the case of those who have not awakened to the True Mind and do not understand the ultimate truth, they can be born in the lowest grade of the highest level in the Realm of True Reward and Adornment if they fulfill the following conditions: 1) they have never slandered the Mahāyāna Dharma, 2) they have a firm belief in the karmic law of cause and effect, and 3) they have aspired to enter the unsurpassed bodhisattva path (Note 1).

It needs to be noted that those born in the lowest grade of the highest level in the Pure Land of Ultimate Bliss have to cultivate the Buddha Dharma for an extremely long time and the fruition they attain is also far inferior to those born in the highest or middle grade of the highest level. Practitioners should keep these differences in mind and weigh their options prudently.

Taking the aforementioned points into consideration, a practitioner who seeks rebirth in the Pure Land of Ultimate Bliss should earnestly practice Buddha-mindfulness through name recitation if no superior method is available. But if he is fortunate enough to come upon a better method, he should definitely pursue it in order to strive for rebirth in the highest grade of the highest level. Please do not be complacent with the lowest or the middle grade of the highest level. The greater the mind, the more expansive the vision; a higher aspiration, as opposed to a louder voice, is what enables one to "behold a grander Buddha."

Moreover, Bodhisattva Mahāsthāmaprāpta's Dharma-door for perfect mastery through Buddha-mindfulness is not the only method that teaches the mindfulness of Buddha's Dharma-body. There are many other Dharma-doors that teach the mindfulness of Buddha's Dharma-body and all of them are signless Buddha-mindfulness in essence. In keeping with the length of this book, I shall cite only a few passages from the *Buddha Treasury Sūtra* (佛藏經) to attest my point:

Śāriputra, what is meant by bearing the Buddha in mind? Seeing that which is without anything is called bearing the Buddha in mind. Śāriputra, Buddhas are unquantifiable [for Buddhas are intangible], inconceivable, and immeasurable; thus the seeing of that which is without anything is called bearing the Buddha in mind, also called non-discrimination. Since all Buddhas are non-

12

discriminating, it is said that the mindfulness of the non-discriminating is bearing the Buddha in mind.[10]

As well, seeing the ultimate reality of all dharmas is called seeing the Buddha. What is called the ultimate reality of all dharmas? All dharmas are ultimately empty and without anything, and the bearing of Buddha in mind should depend upon the dharma that is ultimately empty and without anything. Also, in this dharma, not even the subtlest thought is apprehensible, such is called bearing the Buddha in mind.

Śāriputra, this dharma of bearing the Buddha in mind cuts off the path of language and surpasses all thoughts, in which no thought is apprehensible, such is called the bearing of Buddha in mind. Śāriputra, all thoughts are characterized by quiescence and cessation; to be in accord with such a dharma is called the cultivation of bearing the Buddha in mind.[11]

One should not bear the Buddha in mind relying on any form. Why is that? Thinking of forms leads to the apprehension of appearance, desiring

---

[10] CBETA, T15, no. 653, 785a25: 舍利弗！云何名為念佛？見無所有名為念佛。舍利弗！諸佛無量不可思議、不可稱量，以是義故，見無所有名為念佛。實名無分別，諸佛無分別，以是故言念無分別即是念佛。

[11] CBETA, T15, no. 653, 785a25: 復次，見諸法實相名為見佛。何等名為諸法實相？所謂諸法畢竟空無所有，以是畢竟空無所有法念佛。復次，如是法中，乃至小念尚不可得，是名念佛。舍利弗！是念佛法斷語言道，過出諸念不可得念，是名念佛。

specific qualities breeds discernment. Having neither shape nor appearance, neither conditions nor properties, such is called bearing the Buddha in mind. Hence one should know: the true way of bearing the Buddha in mind is without discrimination, apprehension, and abandonment.[12]

Bearing the Buddha in mind is called the shattering of applied attention and sustained attention toward everything good or ill; it is without applied attention and sustained attention, and is thoughtless and quiescent. Why is that? One should not rely on applied attention and sustained attention to be mindful of Buddha. The absence of applied attention and sustained attention is called the pure way of bearing the Buddha in mind.[13]

You should not attach to even the subtlest thoughts when you bear the Buddha in mind, nor should you develop conceptual proliferations or discriminations. Why is that? All dharmas are empty of an inherent nature; hence, you should not be mindful of any kind of sign. The so-called signlessness is the true way of being mindful of

---

[12] CBETA, T15, no. 653, 785b5: 舍利弗！一切諸念皆寂滅相，隨順是法，此則名為修習念佛。不可以色念佛。何以故？念色取相貪味為識，無形、無色、無緣、無性，是名念佛。是故當知，無有分別、無取、無捨，是真念佛。
[13] T15, no. 653, 785b13: 念佛名為破善不善一切覺觀，無覺無觀寂然無想，名為念佛。何以故？不應以覺觀憶念諸佛，無覺無觀名為清淨念佛。

Buddha.[14]

All of the above excerpts from the *Buddha Treasury Sūtra* describe the state of Buddha-mindfulness in Ultimate Reality (實 相 念 佛). Having realized the True Mind, a practitioner will know that "Buddha" is without physical form and appearance, or any phenomenal characteristic. When this person follows others in chanting Buddha's name, he can say that, "The recitation of Buddha's name encompasses both phenomenon and principle." However, for those who have not yet realized the True Mind, making the same comment frequently and casually constitutes false speech. What accounts for the difference? In the latter case, one has realized neither the phenomena nor the principle of Buddha-mindfulness.

The method of signless Buddha-mindfulness illustrated in this book supplies practitioners with skillful means that can help them progress from sign-dependent to signless mindfulness of Buddha. Some practitioners may also be able to advance to the stage of Buddha-mindfulness in Ultimate Reality in the future when they have accumulated sufficient roots of wisdom and merit.

---

[14] T15, no. 653, 785b13: 汝念佛時莫取小想，莫生戲論、莫有分別。何以故？是法皆空、無有體性、不可念，一相所謂無相，是名真實念佛...。

Chapter 2

The Complementary Nature and the Dual Practice of Chan and Pure Land

2.1 The Complementary Nature of Chan and Pure Land

In this Dharma-ending age, Buddhist practitioners, especially those from the Chan and Pure Land, tend to compare and argue about the superiority of their respective methods of practicing.

Some Chan practitioners think that most Pure Land practitioners seek the truth outside of themselves and beseech blessings from Buddhas and bodhisattvas. Moreover, Chan practitioners think that they also tend to recite the Buddha's name without collecting their mind inwards to explore their intrinsic Buddha-nature. On the other hand, Pure Land practitioners consider their Chan counterparts arrogant and ignorant of the fact that the practice of Buddha-mindfulness can benefit practitioners of all capacities. All of these comments arise from a lack of in-depth understanding of the teachings in the Chan and Pure Land. Sadly, these misunderstandings led to conflicts within Buddhist communities in the form of verbal or written attacks, which have invited scorn and ridicule from outsiders and driven prospective Buddhist learners to take their faith elsewhere. This issue should be taken seriously since the undermining of other's wisdom-life constitutes a transgression of grave consequence.

Master Hongyi (弘一大師) said it rather well: "Not

yielding to the ancients is ambitious, not yielding to the contemporaries is narrow-minded." We should refrain from passing casual, subjective judgment before we acquire a thorough understanding of others' practice, and we should not criticize until we have a chance to study and put into practice their teachings. Only when we have reached a certain level within our actual practice can we venture to comment in private, provided our intent is well-natured.

Many eminent contemporary Buddhist masters and monastics have advocated "the dual practice of Chan and Pure Land" on the ground that the two traditions are compatible and complementary. But some find this perplexing as they believe that Buddha-mindfulness should be practiced by either vocal or mental recitation of the sacred name of Buddha, or visualization of the Buddha's image, whereas the "gateless gate" of Chan is entered by abandoning all signs and characteristics, cutting off the path of language, and ceasing all workings of the mind. So how could the two possibly be compatible with each other and be practiced in combination?

Novice practitioners may harbor such doubts. However, digging deeper, one will realize that all Dharma-doors converge in the end and ultimately there is no difference in their objectives. In fact, it can be said, all practice methods work toward the training of meditative concentration, and all fruitions lead to the realization of pure land. Although the Buddha Dharma is said to contain as many as eighty-four thousand methods of cultivation, each and every one of them converge upon the training of meditative concentration. When one acquires a sufficient degree of meditative concentration, one will be able to comply with and rely upon the four noble truths, the eightfold noble path, the twelvefold chain of dependent arising, the four foundations of mindfulness, as well as the knowledge of ultimate truth to reach the stage of Chan initiation, personally realize one's Buddha-nature, or eliminate one's afflictions.

For those who practice Buddha-mindfulness, this is the course of cultivation to realize Buddha-nature while in this world. The same path is also followed by those who are born in the Pure Land of Ultimate Bliss and bring with them all their karma. They will hear Buddha's teachings after their lotus flowers unfold and subsequently attain the acquiescence to non-arising (*anutpannakṣāntika*; 無生忍) (Note 2). Essentially, the objective of all practice methods is to develop mental absorption.

In a broad sense, all eighty-four thousand Dharma-doors, including those of the Pure Land tradition, are methods to cultivate meditative concentration. A person who has practiced and realized any one of these Dharma-doors will have also realized, to a greater or lesser extent, the Mind-Only Pure Land. If one has reached the stage of adept (*aśaikṣa*; 無學) (Note 3), one would be able to dwell securely in nirvana, which is the true and ultimate pure land. Alternatively, a person who has reached the stage of adept can also choose to take rebirth in any one of the three types of Buddha's pure land, namely, the Realm Inhabited by Both Ordinary and Saints (凡聖同居土), the Realm of Expedients and Remainders (方便有餘土), and the Realm of True Reward and Adornment (實報莊嚴土).

When one reaches the Buddha Ground, one will dwell in the Realm of Eternal Quiescence and Brightness (常寂光淨土). Unlike the three realms mentioned above, it is not a pure land created by Buddha through transformation, but the true and ultimate Mind-Only Pure Land. In summary, Chan contemplation and samādhi training are the means; attainment of the pure lands, the fruition. This

21

understanding should put a lid on all disputes between the Chan and Pure Land traditions.

For a disciple of the Three Jewels, this world offers an environment that is challenging but conducive to speedy progress in the training of meditative contemplation, while the Pure Land of Ultimate Bliss provides an easy, impediment-free setting. Practitioners who have mastered signless Buddha-mindfulness can achieve rebirth in the Pure Land of Ultimate Bliss in one single lifetime. Yet compared to those who cultivate the Buddha Dharma in this world, those who go to the Pure Land have to spend an exceedingly long time to reach the state of ultimate liberation. Since this subject is outside the scope of this book, a discussion is not included here.

2.2 Examples of the Dual Practice of Chan and Pure Land

A Mahāyāna Chan practitioner who has attained ultimate liberation is able to rely on the non-abiding Mind to fulfill the Six Kinds of Mindfulness, namely the mindfulness of Buddha, Dharma, Sangha, giving, precepts, as well as the virtues of celestial beings. Among the Six Kinds of Mindfulness, whether the first and foremost Buddha-mindfulness or the other five, all of them are Pure Land practices in essence. In addition, a Mahāyāna Chan practitioner who has attained ultimate liberation sees the Buddha-nature almost perfectly. Thus he can access Buddha's insights and thereby realize the Mind-Only Pure Land. From both perspectives, Chan and Pure Land share a common ground.

Throughout the history of Buddhism, many Chan masters have advocated the Dharma-door of Buddha-mindfulness for the reason that prostrating to the Buddha and bearing the Buddha in mind are effective entrance expedients for Chan contemplation. At the same time, many Pure Land monasteries encouraged the practice of contemplative Buddha-mindfulness. The illustrious Chan Master Yongming Yanshou (永明延壽; 904–975), for one, promoted the all-unifying ideology of "Principle, Pedagogy, Chan, and Pure Land." Another prominent example is

Changlu Zongze (長蘆宗賾; ? –1107), also known as Master Cijue (慈覺大師), who attained enlightenment through Chan but espoused the dual practice of Chan and Pure Land. Indeed, while Master Cijue authored the ten-volume *Rules of Purity for Chan Monasteries*[15] for the Chan school, he was an even more prolific writer for the Pure Land tradition. In his *A Condensed Account of Pure Land*,[16] he proposed that "although Buddha-mindfulness and Chan contemplation both seek their own tenets, but the principle and objective are the same. Just like there are many rivers and mountains, yet the clouds and the moon above them are the same. And it can be said that a horse can be tethered to any willow and one can get to Chang'an through the gates of all households." [17] The most well-known exponent of combined practice is no doubt Chan Master Yunqi Zhuhong (雲棲袾宏; 1535–1615) of the late Ming Dynasty, reverently referred to as Master Lianchi (Master Lotus Pond; 蓮池大師) by practitioners of Buddha-mindfulness. The inscription on his stupa reads:

> With an alms bowl and a walking stick, [the Master] journeyed extensively to seek out every mentor. North in Mt. Wutai he was blessed to see light shining from Bodhisattva Mañjuśrī, and in Fu'nü, he joined the masses in battling demons. In the capital, he consulted Master Xiaoling Debao, who said to him, "Huh! You travelled three thousand miles to seek my teaching, what teaching do I have?" So he took leave to

---

[15] *Chanyuan Qingqui* 禪苑清規
[16] *Jingtu Jianyaolu* 淨土簡要錄
[17] CBETA, T47, no. 1973, 318b24: 是故念佛參禪各求宗旨。溪山雖異雲月是同。可謂處處綠楊堪繫馬。家家門首透長安。

Dongchang. On his way, upon hearing drum beats from a firewood house, he suddenly attained awakening. After that he wrote a verse:

For twenty years, there was doubt about this matter,
Three thousand miles of journeying lead me to encounter the extraordinary;
Burning incense and throwing spears seem like dreams,
The contention between Buddhas and demons about right and wrong is plainly insignificant.

Thus all doubts evaporated as he awakened to the Dharma of non-attainment.... At first, when the Master started his journey of seeking, he benefited from the practice of contemplative Buddha-mindfulness. When he got to this point, he established the Pure Land tradition and fervently promoted it to assist practitioners of all capacities. He composed the *Commentary on the Amitābha Sūtra*,[18] a work of a hundred thousand words, in which he harmonized phenomena and principle by ascribing the objective of all practices to the Mind-Only. Moreover, he recalled his reading of the *Recorded Sayings of Gaofeng*[19] and said that it was the sharpest instrument for Chan contemplation and that no one could surpass its author's genuine, adamantine achievement. He kept the book with him wherever he went. During that time the Master

---

[18] *Mituo shuchao* 彌陀疏鈔
[19] *Gaofeng yulu* 高峰語錄

was thinking about compiling the teachings of Lushan Huiyuan and Yongming Yanshou, and so he further compiled the apt sayings and vital exchanges of prior Chan luminaries and edited them into a book called *Whip for Spurring Students Onward through the Chan Barrier Check Point*.[20] He had both carved in order to show the key of Chan contemplation and to highlight the fact that the dual cultivation of Chan and Pure Land is not something outside of the one Mind.[21]

According to the inscription, Master Lianchi first honed his skill by way of contemplative Buddha-mindfulness and later on gained insight into the "principle" through Chan contemplation. Because of this, he proposed a combined practice of Chan and Pure Land and wrote the *Commentary on the Amitābha Sūtra*, a work of a hundred thousand words held in high regard by Pure Land practitioners. As for the other acclaimed work of his, *Whip for Spurring Students Onward through the Chan Barrier Check Point*, it is said that "throughout his entire life, he kept it in his sack when he was on the road and on his desk when he was not. One glimpse of it sufficed to embolden and inspire him,

---

[20] *Changuan cejin* 禪關策進
[21] CBETA, J33, no. B277, vol. 25, 194b12: 即單瓢隻杖遊諸方。遍參知識。。至伏牛。隨眾煉魔。入京師。參遍融笑巖二大老。皆有開發。過東昌。忽有悟。作偈曰。二十年前事可疑。三千里外遇何奇。焚香擲戟渾如夢。魔佛空爭是與非。乘悟併消。歸無所得...初師發足操方。從參究念佛得力。至是遂開淨土一門。普攝三根。極力主張。乃著彌陀疏鈔十萬餘言。融會事理。指歸唯心。又憶昔見高峰語錄。謂自來參究此事。最極精銳。無逾此師之純鋼鑄就者。向懷之行腳。唯時師意併匡山永明而一之。更錄古德機緣中喫緊語編之。曰禪關策進。併刻之。以示參究之訣。蓋顯禪淨雙修。不出一心。

impelling him to press forward in his cultivation."[22] Indeed, throughout his life, Master Lianchi urged himself to work hard in accordance with the teachings in *Whip for Spurring Students Onward through the Chan Barrier Check Point* in order to reach the state of ultimate liberation. This monumental work has received paramount plaudit from Chan practitioners of later generations.

As for Yunqi Zhuhong, he, with his insights of a Chan master, advocated the joint practice of Chan and Pure Land. Not only did he promote Buddha-mindfulness through name recitation, calling it the "abiding within phenomena," he also advocated the practice of contemplative Buddha-mindfulness using the interrogative "Who is bearing the Buddha in mind?" regarding it as the "abiding within principle." What this eminent Pure Land patriarch taught was precisely a synthesis of Chan and Pure Land. Chan Master Yongming Yanshou, who came before Zhuhong, was an exponent of this dual practice as well. Based upon his cultivation and realization as a Chan master, Yongming Yanshou too understood very well that Chan and Pure Land are interconnected because the objective of all Dharma-doors boils down to the cultivation of meditative concentration and all achievements of Dharma cultivation are essentially of the Pure Land.

---

[22] *Changuan cejin* 禪關策進: CBETA, T48, no. 2024, vol. 1, 1097c15

2.3 An Overview of the Dual Practice of Chan and Pure Land

Most people practice Buddha-mindfulness by reciting Buddha's name with a scattered mind; they may think they are being mindful of Buddha, but their minds are actually unfocused and constantly giving way to deluded thoughts. The more serious kind of practitioners will quickly return to the recitation of Buddha's name as soon as they realize that their minds have drifted off. As for the most conscientious practitioners, they will not only mentally recite Buddha's name but also bear a thought of Buddha in mind during their practice. Eventually, they will advance to the stage of signless mindfulness of Buddha, in which the thought of Buddha persists but Buddha's name no longer arises, and they would be able to carry out such signless mindfulness of Buddha alongside daily activities. They are essentially "reciting Buddha's name till there is no name to be recited," as a common saying goes. This level of meditative concentration corresponds to the beginning practice of Bodhisattva Mahāsthāmaprāpta's Dharma-door for perfect mastery through Buddha-mindfulness.

At this stage, a practitioner achieves undisturbed one-pointed absorption by abiding in a continuous pure thought of Buddha free of image or name. As the mindfulness of Buddha goes on continuously, he will experience Dharma-joy accompanied by remarkable ease and composure. By now he will also be able to contemplate Chan. He can guard and contemplate a *huatou* (or a *gong'an*). As you can see, Pure Land and Chan can be seamlessly woven together.

After mastering the signless mindfulness of Buddha via the aids of prostration to Buddha and recitation of Buddha's name, if a practitioner of Buddha-mindfulness seeks to cultivate the Great Śūraṅgama Samādhi (楞嚴大定), he must acquire knowledge of meditative concentration and carefully read the *Śūraṅgama Sūtra*. On top of that, he needs to carry out signless mindfulness of Buddha amidst all daily activities as well as during regular, daily meditation sessions. Once he has eliminated his hindrances in terms of phenomena and principle, he will be able to gradually enter deep into the Great Śūraṅgama Samādhi and hence realize the many kinds of Buddha-Mindfulness Samādhi (Note 4).

Some practitioners of Buddha-mindfulness or mantra chanting recite a Buddha's name or a specific mantra during everyday life and set aside one or two hours at a fixed time each day for meditation. They join their palms or make a hand seal (*mudra*) while chanting Buddha's name or a mantra. Initially, they listen to their own steady-paced chanting with unbroken mindfulness. As their proficiency in meditative concentration improves, their scattered mind will unify with the recitation and reach a state of serenity and imperturbability.

Upon reaching this stage, a practitioner with sufficient knowledge of meditative concentration would continue the chanting but stop paying attention to the sound of Buddha's name or the mantra. He would as a result slowly slip into a state of samādhi (you are unaware of entering into this state of mental absorption until you have exited from it) wherein the perception of time and space disappears. During this time, although oral recitation goes on, his mind has already settled in a state of deep mental absorption.

In some cases, a practitioner goes from oral chanting of Buddha's name to silent mental recitation accompanied by mindful self-listening. He then ceases the mental recitation altogether when his mind becomes unified and settled in the continuous thought of Buddha, eventually slipping into a state of samādhi. But regardless of which of the above routes one takes, one can only enter this state of mental absorption if and only if one possesses sufficient power of meditative concentration and a sound understanding of its cultivation. At this level, Pure Land practices cross over into Chan.

The scenarios I have described above is limited to the practice of meditative concentration and the state of "one-pointed absorption within phenomena (事一心)." As for "one-pointed absorption within principle (理一心)," as the term itself suggests, it is a state that corresponds with the direct perception of one's intrinsic Buddha-nature (self-nature). As the saying goes, "The Western Pure Land is not even an inch away and the Buddha is none but one's self-nature." This spontaneous realization of the intrinsic Buddha, which is the state of the Mind-Only Pure Land, is what one awakens to in Chan. In truth, by no other means can one attain this realization except through the combined practice of Chan and Pure Land. Whether one personally realizes the ultimate truth through the contemplation of a *huatou*, a *gong'an*, a sharp prod (機鋒), or contemplative Buddha-mindfulness, the nature of this process is Chan and nothing but Chan. There are many different ways to initiate Chan, but the state to which one is enlightened upon seeing the path as well as the process of contemplation to reach it are nonetheless identical. Therefore, Chan and Pure Land should not be divorced into two separate traditions since they complement each other and are mutually reinforcing. The following passage from Vol. 3 of Chan Master Yunqi Zhuhong's *Commentary on the Amitābha Sūtra* gives a general description on this subject:

> Experiential investigation refers not just to the mindfulness of Buddha upon hearing the chanting of his name but also an instantaneous introspection and examination of the origin of this chanting. During its consummation, experiential investigation results in sudden correspondence to one's fundamental mind. This mind [that investigates] can be called existent, yet this mind that can recollect is empty of any inherent nature and the Buddha being recollected is not apprehensible. It can be called nonexistent, yet this mind that can recollect is always pristine and aware, and the Buddha being recollected is clear and distinct. If this mind is said to be both existent and nonexistent, then the concepts of the presence and absence of thought will vanish. If it is said to be neither existent nor non-existent, then the concepts of the presence and absence of thought are both retained. Nonexistence entails permanent quiescence, not nonexistence entails permanent illumination. [To the contrary,] as the one mind is not "both

existent and non-existent" nor "neither existent nor non-existent," it is therefore neither quiescence nor illumination and yet both quiescence and illumination. Being the only mind, it is void of verbalization and conception, and completely eludes description. Having witnessed this truth, one is said to have achieved one-pointed absorption within principle. [The witnessing of this truth] leads to wisdom, as it illumines the illusory; it encompasses samādhi, as it illumines the inherent emptiness of the illusory and the illusory would be naturally subdued. The illumination not only subdues the illusory but can also shatter it.[23]

It also reads:

It is unnecessary to differentiate the words "contemplation" and "doubt." Doubt is just another expression of contemplation; both refer to direct experience and investigation. Simply guard the *huatou* "Who is bearing the Buddha in mind?" following the principle of achieving

---

[23] CEBTA, J22, no. 424, vol. 3, 661c12: 體究者，聞佛名號，不惟憶念；即令返觀，體察究審，鞫其根源。體究之極，於自本心，忽然契合。若言其有，則能念之心，本體自空；所念之佛，了不可得。若言其無，則能念之心，靈靈不昧；所念之佛，歷歷分明。若言其亦有亦無，則有念無念俱泯。若言非有非無，則有念無念俱存。非有則常寂，非無則常照。非雙亦，非雙非，則不寂不照，而照而寂。言思路絕，無可名狀，故唯一心。以見諦故，名理一心也。言慧者，能照妄故。兼定者，照妄本空，妄自伏故。又照能破妄，不但伏故。

awakening. The ancients said, "When one guards the *huatou*, one should not speculate and force an interpretation, nor should one discard all aside. One should simply keep guarding it. This is the key.[24]

The excerpts above are Master Yunqi Zhuhong's (Master Lianchi) instruction on Buddha-mindfulness through contemplation or experiential investigation. The whole process—beginning with the contemplation of "Who is bearing the Buddha in mind?" until the moment of awakening—clearly illustrates the intimate relationship between the practices of Chan and Pure Land.

Whether one realizes the True Mind through Buddha-mindfulness or Chan contemplation, the nature of the process itself is essentially that of Chan. And in the same vein, whether one realizes the True Mind through Buddha-mindfulness in this world or upon hearing the Dharma teachings of Buddha and bodhisattvas in the Pure Land of Ultimate Bliss, the essence of the realization is also nothing but Chan. In either case, the state that one realizes upon awakening is totally identical.

---

[24] CBETA, J33, no. B277, vol. 21, 149b2: 參疑二字，不必分解。疑則參之別名，總是體究追審之意。但看「念佛是誰」，以悟為則而已。又古人云：看話頭，不得卜度穿鑿，亦不得拋向無事甲裏。但只恁麼看。此要言也。

Chapter 3

Essential Knowledge for the Cultivation of Bodhisattva Mahāsthāmaprāpta's Dharma-Door for Perfect Mastery through Buddha-Mindfulness

3.1 A Dharma-Door for the Cultivation of Meditative Concentration rather than Recitation of Buddha's Name

Bodhisattva Mahāsthāmaprāpta's Dharma-door for perfect mastery through Buddha-mindfulness is a method of samādhi training. It is a direct and effective way to accomplish the Pure Land Dharma-door by way of samādhi cultivation (Note 5).

Most Pure Land practitioners cultivate Buddha-mindfulness by invoking Buddha's name. They recite a Buddha's name either orally or mentally until no discursive thoughts arise in mind except the name of Buddha, a state of mental absorption referred to as "one-pointed absorption within phenomena." This course of cultivation applies to mantra chanters as well.

The twenty-five Dharma-doors for perfect mastery of Dharma cultivation expounded by the twenty-five bodhisattvas in the *Śūraṅgama Sūtra* are geared toward the training of meditative concentration. Each of them enables the practitioner to directly perceive the Buddha-nature, attain "one-pointed absorption within principle," or even the state of ultimate liberation by realizing the emptiness of the five-aggregates—hence the appellation "Dharma-doors for perfect mastery." Among these twenty-five methods, the twenty-fourth one is the Dharma-door for perfect mastery through Buddha-mindfulness put forth by Bodhisattva Mahāsthāmaprāpta. In his illustration of this Dharma-door, Bodhisattva Mahāsthāmaprāpta makes no reference to the recitation of Buddha's name anywhere. He uses the words "recollect" and "be mindful of" throughout the description of his choice method, and never once mentions the "reciting" or "chanting" of Buddha's name. Toward the end, the Bodhisattva states that one can "enter samādhi" by "reining in all six sense faculties and abiding in one continuous pure thought."

Why is there no mentioning of the recitation of Buddha's name? Because the recollection and mindfulness of something are not contingent upon the presence of names, images, or sounds. If there are names and sounds, one would be reciting and chanting Buddha's name instead. This is the reason that Bodhisattva Mahāsthāmaprāpta's explanation of his method of Buddha-mindfulness makes no reference at all to the recitation of Buddha's name, but only the recollection and mindfulness of Buddha.

During oral recitation of Buddha's name, the tongue has to move to produce sound. At the same time, the muscles of the chest and abdomen have to expand and contract to enable exhalation and quick inhalation, which means that the body and the nose are both active. When one listens attentively to one's own chanting, the ears are involved. Since the five sense faculties are all fully engaged in this process, the mental faculty (*manas*)[25] has to participate in

---

[25] The mental faculty, or *manas* in Sanskrit, is one of the six sense faculties, but unlike the first five sense faculties, it is a mental entity unassociated with a physical organ. The six sense faculties and their six corresponding sense objects are essential conditions for the arising of the six consciousnesses; the *manas* is called the mental faculty as it is

the process as well. What this means is that when one is chanting Buddha's name, one cannot possibly "rein in all six sense faculties," let alone "abide in one continuous pure thought."

When a practitioner recites Buddha's name silently in mind while being mindful of Buddha, although his five sense faculties—visual, auditory, olfactory, gustatory, and tactile—are not engaged, the mental faculty still needs to partake in the process nonetheless. This is because when one is repeatedly reciting Buddha's name in mind, one is continuously bringing forth a few simple but distracting thoughts. For instance, if one practices with Buddha Amitābha, then with each mental recitation of the Buddha's name, four syllables, which are four thoughts, are being continuously repeated in one's mind. Insofar as there are four thoughts recurring in the mind, the mental faculty is not being held in an unstirred state. When the mental faculty is not being held in continuous, one-pointed focus, one is not "reining in all six sense faculties and abiding in one continuous pure thought."

"Abiding in one continuous pure thought" connotes the one thought held in mind being of a pure nature. Thoughts about worldly matters are not pure thoughts, even thoughts about virtuous acts or the Buddha Dharma are not considered pure either. In terms of the cultivation of meditative concentration, any thoughts that come with language, symbols, or images are considered deluded and impure. The recollection and mindfulness of Buddha can only be deemed pure if the thought of Buddha is free of them. Only when one can bear such a pure thought of

---

required for the arising of the mental consciousness (*manovijñāna*). It should be noted that in addition to being a sense faculty, the *manas* is also one of the eight forms of consciousness (see footnote 26).

Buddha in mind without interruption can one be considered as "abiding in one continuous pure thought." If this pure thought is dropped and picked up again and again, one is not "abiding in one continuous pure thought" but merely bearing a pure thought intermittently, even if the interruption lasted only one or half a second. Essentially, to "enter samādhi," one needs to be able to not only "rein in all six sense faculties" but also "abide in one continuous pure thought." The fulfillment of these two conditions specifically point to a state free of any signs. Here's a passage from the *Mahāratnakūṭa Sūtra* (大寶積經) that illustrates my point:

> Signlessness refers to the absence of individual body and its designations, and the absence of words and sentences, as well as appearances.[26]

This concept of signlessness is one that all practitioners who cultivate Bodhisattva Mahāsthāmaprāpta's Dharma-door for perfect mastery through Buddha-mindfulness ought to understand thoroughly.

The word "signless" designates the literal absence of physical body as well as all knowable and perceivable characteristics that spawn from its existence, such as thoughts, logic, language, letters, words, sentences, or any visible or perceivable expressions of meaning.

To go deeper, in this physical world that we inhabit, there are humans, all kinds of organisms and species, non-sentient life forms, as well as life forms whose existence lie in a murky zone between sentient and non-sentient (the realms of celestial beings, asuras, hell beings, and hungry

---

[26] CEBTA, T11, no. 310, vol. 4, 23a15: 言無相者，所謂無身及身施設，無名無句亦無示現。

ghosts are not taken into consideration here). All these life forms exhibit a wide range of differences not only from one another but even among their own kind. Human beings are all different from one another in terms of physical appearance, for example. The differences between sentient and non-sentient beings or among members of the same species stem from the existence of the physical body, without which there would be no visible characteristics. Therefore, the absence of visible characteristics is the absence of signs.

Moreover, the presence of all visible characteristics, behavior, symbols, thinking, and rules in this material world is predicated on the existence of the physical body. Without the existence of a physical body in the material world, all visible characteristics would disappear along with it. When there are no body as well as any visible characteristic, there would not be any behavior, symbol, language, thinking, rule, and so forth to speak of. This is also true of the heavenly worlds of the desire realm (Note 6), the plane of existence regarded as heaven or the kingdom of god in non-Buddhist religions.

Furthermore, the diverse forms of linguistic expressions in this material world, including the communicative sounds and signals of animals, are predicated upon the existence of a physical body as well. Language allows communication of meaning with the same or even different species and the formation of words and sentences gives rise to thoughts and ideas. With thinking comes logic and reasoning, which evolve into the mundane bodies of knowledge such as literature, theology, science, art, metaphysics, and so on. In addition, the existence of physical body is also the root cause of craving and disputes, which necessitate the establishment of guidelines to settle disagreements engendered by conflicts of interests. Over time, these guidelines develop into laws and regulations.

In summary, the generation, continued presence, and evolution of the dharma characteristics of languages, sentences, terminologies, thinking, and rules are all grounded in the existence of the physical body. And these phenomena exist for one and one purpose only: communication; for the need to communicate would not exist if there were no physical body in the first place. Again, this is true both in our physical world and in the six heavenly abodes of the desire realm.

As a matter of fact, most Buddhas manifest their attainment of Buddhahood in the human world rather than in the heavens of the desire realm. Celestial beings (the various kinds of heavenly beings and their lords) residing in the heavens of the desire realm are very difficult to enlighten because they are deeply attached to the pleasures of the five senses. As for human beings, it would be difficult for Buddhas to guide them into the Buddha Dharma if Buddhas do not manifest themselves in the human world. When a Buddha manifests his attainment of Buddhahood in the human world, the World-Honored One can be seen and heard by humans, and at the same time, celestial beings of the realms of desire and form can also come down and pay homage to the World-Honored One in the human world if they are inclined to the learning of the Dharma. Last but not least, all Buddhas attain Buddhahood in the human world because it is a world in which they can manifest themselves in physical form and infuse their teachings using the physical form-derived instruments of language, reasoning, principle, and so forth.

The above explanations are meant to illustrate and clarify that signlessness describes the absence of a physical body, its derivative features, written and spoken language, or any expression of meaning. By the same token, in

Bodhisattva Mahāsthāmaprāpta's teaching of the Dharma-door for perfect mastery through Buddha-mindfulness, "recollecting and being mindful of Buddha" and "reining in all six sense faculties and abiding in one continuous pure thought" refer to a signless mental state that cannot be shown to others. Unless one explains what this mental state entails through the use of one's body as well as spoken and written words, which are logic and rules derived from the existence of the body, it is impossible for another person to comprehend its essence and the way to achieve it. Though difficult to understand, this mental state of signless mindfulness of Buddha is the true essence of Bodhisattva Mahāsthāmaprāpta's Dharma-door for perfect mastery through Buddha-mindfulness.

3.2 Clarification and Encouragement

The amount of time it takes to master signless mindfulness of Buddha depends entirely on one's understanding of its underlying concepts as detailed in this book and whether one practices accordingly. Practitioners who have fully understood the content of this book and practice accordingly could accomplish this Dharma-door in roughly two to six months. Those who are of a sharp capacity or already possess sufficient power of in-motion meditative concentration can master it the moment they hear it.

On September 3, 1991, I started lecturing on this practice method to thirty practitioners at two locations: the Chan center of a financial institution in Taipei and the Chan hall of Mr. and Mrs. Chen in Shipai (Taipei). Of the thirty practitioners, two accomplished this practice of signless mindfulness in six weeks and more people continued to have success after them. Among those who have accomplished this Dharma-door, those from the Shipai group accounted for a larger share. They owed their success to their putting of what they had learned into actual practice. Although this group of practitioners started learning the Buddha Dharma relatively late and hence took longer time to understand the practice method, their faith and diligence enabled them to accomplish it within three months. Later on, a few people mastered the practice in three months after listening to the recording of my lectures and reading my essay "On Signless Buddha-Prostration and Buddha-Mindfulness." So, within the last quarter of that year [1991], a total of nine people mastered this Dharma-door. Some had attended my lectures but had yet become skilled in signless mindfulness of Buddha. I found that the reason of their lack of progress was a dislike of the entrance expedients of this Dharma-door, namely, prostration to Buddha and recitation of Buddha's name. As a result, they did not go through with the actual practice.

In the summer of 1989, I presented my short essay "On Signless Buddha-Prostration and Buddha-Mindfulness" as a gift to several lay practitioners of Chan at a Buddhist monastery. Some of them were uninterested in prostration to Buddha and left the essay at the monastery. Some time later, a person with abundant wholesome roots received a newsletter from this monastery and gladly found my essay between the pages. He read it with great delight, practiced accordingly, and became proficient in signless Buddha-mindfulness. He then became able to contemplate *huatou* and was constantly seized by the "sense of doubt (疑情)." He was the first person who mastered signless mindfulness of Buddha simply by reading a short article.

As for regular practitioners of the Pure Land, I urge you to read this book carefully and patiently. Please do not give up trying this Dharma-door simply because the mental state of signless mindfulness seems unimaginable or extremely difficult to achieve. As mentioned earlier, those who had mastered this Dharma-door were mostly Pure Land practitioners who used to recite Buddha's name, and their success is a clear and unmistakable indication that Pure Land practitioners share a strong affinity with this Dharma-door taught by Bodhisattva Mahāsthāmaprāpta. If you have already become proficiency in the reciting of Buddha's name, this would be a perfect method for you and you would enjoy great advantage over those who have never practiced recitation. Once you have mastered this Dharma-door and can maintain your proficiency, you will be confident about gaining rebirth in the Pure Land of Ultimate Bliss at the end of your life.

As of today (February 5, 1992; the second day of the first lunar month), twelve among the thirty practitioners from the two aforementioned practice groups have mastered signless Buddha-mindfulness. Six of them have entered the stage of *huatou* contemplation, among whom four people are constantly seized by the sense of doubt. Out of these six people, only one was originally a Chan practitioner; the other five were all practitioners of name recitation.

As for the other six people who have not started to contemplate Chan but are continuing on their practice of signless Buddha-mindfulness, they too were originally practitioners of name recitation. Now, some of them plan to continue their practice of signless Buddha-mindfulness for the rest of their lives in order to enter deep into Bodhisattva Mahāsthāmaprāpta's Dharma-door for perfect mastery through Buddha-mindfulness, in the hope of attaining rebirth in the Pure Land of Ultimate Bliss. Others would like to continue to strengthen their power of in-motion meditative concentration via prostration to Buddha with signless mindfulness before they are ready to embark on Chan contemplation. Still others choose to practice contemplative Buddha-mindfulness. Among these six practitioners, most of them are seized by the sense of doubt from time to time. Thus, they have turned their practice to contemplative Buddha-mindfulness and hence have occasionally entered the stage of Chan observation. I urge all Buddhist practitioners to look into this practice, as their examples demonstrate that the power of in-motion meditative concentration acquired through signless mindfulness of Buddha is highly useful for both Chan and Pure Land practitioners. As for those who have not yet mastered signless Buddha-mindfulness, they have started to practice it as their faith in it has ripened. All of them are making good progress at the moment.

To summarize, whether you are a Pure Land or a Chan practitioner, so long as you are willing to acquire a sound understanding of the practice steps and essential knowledge of signless Buddha-mindfulness by reading this book and put what you learn into consistent daily practice, you could accomplish this Dharma-door within two to six months. On the contrary, without due diligence and continued practice, it is impossible to achieve proficiency.

3.3 Fundamental Knowledge, Part 1: Essence of the Dharma-Door for Perfect Mastery through Buddha-Mindfulness

Why is Bodhisattva Mahāsthāmaprāpta's Dharma-door of Buddha-mindfulness a practice based on signlessness? To make sure that practitioners can attain the state described in this Dharma-door via correct practices, I will first laid down the fundamental knowledge essential to its practice before going into the various expedient means that aid its cultivation. Please patiently pay close attention to these sections and try to acquire full and thorough understanding of its underlying principles to avoid wasting time and effort practicing incorrectly.

Bodhisattva Mahāsthāmaprāpta's Dharma-door of Buddha-mindfulness should be cultivated through mental recollection rather than oral recitation. At the Śūraṅgama assembly, Bodhisattva Mahāsthāmaprāpta spoke at the request of the Buddha about his Dharma-door for mastery in the following words:

> I remember when, as many aeons ago as there are grains of sand in the Ganges, a Buddha called Infinite Light appeared in the world. In that same

aeon, there were twelve successive Tathāgatas; the last was called Light Surpassing the Sun and Moon. That Buddha taught me the Buddha-Mindfulness Samādhi.

If a person yearns for someone who is oblivious of the other, they will not take notice of nor recognize each other when they meet. If two people yearn for each other with deep affection, then life after life they will be together like a form and its shadow, and will never be apart.

Out of pity for sentient beings, the Tathāgatas of the ten directions are mindful of sentient beings as a mother yearns for her child. If the child runs away, of what use is the mother's regard? But if this child yearns for his mother in the same way that she yearns for him, then life after life they will not be far apart. If sentient beings recollect and are mindful of Buddha, certainly they will see the Buddha now or in the future. They will never be far from the Buddha, and their minds will spontaneously awaken to the True Mind without employing skillful means.

A person who has been near incense will bear its fragrance; it is the same in the case above and is called the adornment of fragrant light.

On the causal ground, I entered the acquiescence to the non-arising with a mind that yearns for Buddha. Now in this world I gather all those who yearn for the Buddha and bring them back to the Pure Land. The Buddha asks about perfect mastery. I would select no other method than this: rein in all six sense faculties and abide in one continuous pure thought to enter samādhi. This is the foremost method.[27]

In this passage, Bodhisattva Mahāsthāmaprāpta states that he had been cultivating the Buddha-Mindfulness Samādhi taught by Buddha Light Surpassing the Sun and Moon incalculable eons ago. Though he was already a final-stage Bodhisattva at the Śūraṅgama assembly, he continued to practice this method and used it to help sentient beings gain rebirth in the pure lands of various Buddhas. In this short description of the Dharma-door for perfect mastery through Buddha-mindfulness, the words "yearn for" and "be mindful of" appear throughout the text, while there is no mention of name recitation. This indicates that the method is definitely not about the recitation of Buddha's name. This is the first point that I would like to clarify and emphasize.

The Buddha expounded the *Śūraṅgama Sūtra* to teach sentient beings the ways to attain ultimate liberation by realizing the emptiness of the five aggregates through the cultivation of the Great Śūraṅgama Samādhi. Therefore, in the sūtra the Buddha first elucidated and explored the

---

[27] CBETA, T19, no. 945, vol. 5, 128a21: 我憶往昔恒河沙劫，有佛出世名無量光，十二如來相繼一劫，其最後佛名超日月光，彼佛教我念佛三昧。譬如有人，一專為憶一人專忘，如是二人若逢不逢、或見非見，二人相憶二憶念深，如是乃至從生至生，同於形影不相乖異，十方如來憐念眾生如母憶子，若子逃逝雖憶何為？子若憶母如母憶時，母子歷生不相違遠，若眾生心憶佛念佛，現前當來必定見佛去佛不遠，不假方便自得心開，如染香人身有香氣，此則名曰香光莊嚴。我本因地以念佛心入無生忍，今於此界攝念佛人歸於淨土。佛問圓通，我無選擇，都攝六根，淨念相繼得三摩地斯為第一！

nature of the True Mind and demonstrated seven futile attempts to locate it. The World-Honored One then asked the twenty-five bodhisattvas to describe their chosen ways of cultivating the Great Śūraṅgama Samādhi and invited Bodhisattva Mañjuśrī to comment on those methods. Lastly, the Buddha delineated the boundaries of the five aggregates and explained the state of realizing their emptiness.

If Bodhisattva Mahāsthāmaprāpta's Dharma-door were that of Buddha-mindfulness through the recitation of Buddha's name, then the cultivation objective would be to achieve undisturbed one-pointed mental focus based on faith, vows, and action such that one can attain rebirth in Buddhas' pure lands. It would be entirely unnecessary for the Buddha to start lecturing in great length on the nature of the True Mind, the delineations of the boundaries of the five aggregates, namely the aggregates of form, sensation, perception, formation and consciousness,[28] and the state of

---

[28] In Buddhism, "consciousness" is the translation of the Sanskrit word *vijñāna*, which denotes awareness, perception, and discernment, or a mind entity that can discern the characteristics of a perceived object. Each sentient being possesses eight forms of consciousness: the five sensory consciousnesses (visual, auditory, olfactory, gustatory, and tactile), the sixth consciousness (*manovijñāna*; the mental consciousness), the seventh (*manas*), as well as the eighth consciousness. The eighth consciousness, also known as the *alayavijñāna*, storehouse consciousness, and the *tathāgatagarbha*, is the fundamental cause of all phenomena. Here, the "aggregate of consciousness" refers collectively to the first six of the eight consciousnesses. What most people regard as the conscious mind is only the mental consciousness—one of the constituent of the consciousness aggregate—since its wide range of functions, such as discrimination, deliberation, recollection, and self-awareness are most familiar to us. A sentient being is said to be a conglomeration of the five aggregates, or constituents, of form, sensation, perception, formation, and consciousness. This classification schema of sentient

realizing their emptiness. Yet, the Buddha not only delivered discourses on these subjects with abundant explanations and illustrations, but also exhorted bodhisattvas to discern and distinguish the aberrant states induced by *māras*. Evidently, this Dharma-door is a Pure Land practice based on samādhi training rather than on the recitation of Buddha's name. This is the second point that I would like to clarify and emphasize.

In the sūtra, Bodhisattva Mahāsthāmaprāpta says, "I entered the acquiescence to the non-arising with a mind that yearns for the Buddha." This means that the Bodhisattva used a method that stills the mind to a one-pointed absorption directly by way of bearing the Buddha in mind, until he was able to "rein in all six sense faculties and abide in one continuous pure thought." As such the Bodhisattva was able to enter deep into the Great Śūraṅgama Samādhi and hence attained the acquiescence to the non-arising of dharmas. These attainments are impossible to achieve by recitation of Buddha's name, unless one switches from Buddha-mindfulness through recitation of Buddha's name to this method of signless recollection of Buddha. This is the third point that I would like to make.

The three points I made above are further explained respectively as follows:

1. Bodhisattva Mahāsthāmaprāpta says: "...Tathāgatas of the ten directions are mindful of sentient beings as a mother yearns for her child. If the child runs away, of what use is the mother's regard? But if the child yearns for his mother in the same way that she yearns for him, then life after life they will not be far apart. If

---

existence is one of the most commonly used system in Buddhism.

living beings recollect and be mindful of Buddha, certainly they will see Buddha now or in the future. They will never be far from Buddha..."

Note that the words "yearn for" recur in this passage and that the analogy of a mother and her son missing each other is used to illustrate the yearning. Suppose you left home as a youth and have been separated from your mother for decades, when you yearn for your mother, her name does not appear in your thought and you do not repeat the word "mother" in your mind all the time. Instead, the longing for your loving mother is a wordless thought of her. Similarly, if you are a parent who misses your children who are studying or living abroad, you miss them in a lingering thought rather than constantly repeating their names in your mind. Or when young couples are in love, they sorely miss each other day and night incessantly when they are apart. Again, they do not repeat each other's names in their minds but simply think about each other constantly. Sometimes, they are so deeply absorbed in the thought of their lover that they become oblivious of the external world. Such wordless yearning is the essence of Bodhisattva Mahāsthāmaprāpta's Dharma-door for perfect mastery through Buddha-mindfulness.

When we hold the thought of one Buddha or one bodhisattva in mind without name, sound, or image but with only a single pure thought, we are essentially "reining in all six sense faculties and abiding in one continuous pure thought." Given how direct and simple this method is, why would one insist on practicing the more complicated method of name recitation? This is why throughout the description of the Dharma-door of Buddha-mindfulness, there is not a single word about chanting Buddha's name but repeated emphasis on the yearning and mindfulness of Buddha. Understandably, if this Dharma-door employs the recitation of Buddha's name, there would have been explicit references to it, as in the *Amitābha Sūtra*, among others, which states clearly that one can take rebirth in the pure land by single-mindedly chanting Buddha's name for a particular number of days, or single-mindedly chanting Buddha's name for a certain number of thoughts at the end of current life. Thus, "recollection" and "mindfulness" are the crux of this Dharma-door.

If a virtuous, knowledgeable Buddhist teacher interprets this Dharma-door as that of the recitation of Buddha's name, he must be using it as an introductory means. When the time is right, he will certainly introduce his students to the cultivation of signless Buddha-mindfulness, the essence of Bodhisattva Mahāsthāmaprāpta's Dharma-door of Buddha-mindfulness. Practitioners who cultivate this Dharma-door with solid skill in the recitation of Buddha's name can quickly subdue their six sense faculties, experience Dharma-joy, and practice signless mindfulness with merriment.

2. Secondly, in the *Śūraṅgama Sūtra*, the Buddha delivered an extensive discourse for Venerable Ananda and the others to elucidate and explore the nature of the True Mind in the so-called episode of "the seven futile attempts to locate the True Mind." After making the disciples understood the inherent

emptiness of the illusory minds, the Buddha ordered the twenty-five adept bodhisattvas to recount their respective ways of mastering the Great Śūraṅgama Samādhi. Then, Bodhisattva Mañjuśrī, the number one in wisdom and the Teacher of seven Buddhas of the past, commented on which of these twenty-five methods is most suitable for sentient beings in this world and concluded that it is Bodhisattva Avalokiteśvara's Dharma-door for perfect mastery through the ear faculty. Then, the Buddha expounded the Four Instructions on Pure and Wise Conduct (四種清淨明誨), and went into great detail about how, during the cultivation of meditative concentration, to delineate the domain of the form aggregate and realize its emptiness. The same instructions were also given with respect to the delineation of the aggregates of sensation, perception, formation, and consciousness, as well as on how to realize their emptiness. Subsequently, the Buddha taught the disciples how to discern and distinguish the aberrant states induced by *māras*.

If the *Śūraṅgama Sūtra*'s teachings were on how to attain rebirth in the countless pure lands of Buddhas through the recitation of Buddha's name, then there would have been no need for the Buddha to deliver a lengthy discourse on these profound notions. The World-Honored One would have simply talked about the magnificence of the pure lands and how to achieve rebirth there by way of vow-making and reciting Buddha's name with one-pointed focus. The absence of these contents shows that all twenty-five Dharma-doors set forth in the *Śūraṅgama Sūtra* are ways to cultivate the Great Śūraṅgama Samādhi.

Among them, the Dharma-door of Buddha-mindfulness is considered the second best to the Dharma-door for the mastery through the ear faculty for samādhi cultivation and Chan initiation. This Dharma-door, therefore, is the direct way to cultivate the ultimate, Mind-Only Pure Land via samādhi training.

Before the industrial revolution, people enjoyed a simple livelihood in agrarian societies. They started off to the fields at dawn and returned home at dusk. Free time was abundant except during the harvest season and population was fairly sparse. A few miles outside the town, the bustling noise was replaced by the sounds of the countryside. In this kind of living environment where one can find seclusion under the trees or alongside a brook, the Dharma-door for perfect mastery through the ear faculty is certainly the perfect way of cultivation. Our modern life today cannot be more different from that kind of agrarian living. Many people leave for work before daybreak and work a hectic schedule until late night. You can hardly find a quiet spot even if you go deep into the mountains. It is no longer possible to cultivate the Dharma-door of the ear faculty given both the scarcity of time and our living conditions.

Moreover, if one has mastered both the Dharma-doors for perfect mastery through the ear faculty and Buddha-mindfulness, one will see that neither method is superior to the other since their ultimate goal is identical. Personally, I find the latter a more straightforward practice method than the former, especially for modern people who are deprived of the bucolic sounds of nature.

The Dharma-door for perfect mastery through the ear faculty depends on the ear's function to receive sound. One starts by listening to sounds attentively in meditation to keep one's mind from grasping external states, until the sounds simply pass through one's ears without being retained. As one's mind turns inward and becomes quiescent, one advances from "entering the flow" to the "extinguishing of sensory objects." In other words, the hearer is no longer chasing the source of the sounds—sounds are simply sounds, the hearer remains the hearer who is settled in the quiescent internal state of an unstirred mind. At this point, one is said to have reined in the ear faculty and retreated to the mental faculty. In other words, the listening to sounds only serves the purpose of eliminating distraction. Eventually, all cultivation methods (i.e. the cultivation of inner knowledge and meditative concentration) have to get to the mental faculty.

Bodhisattva Avalokiteśvara's Dharma-door for perfect mastery through the ear faculty is well suited for the agrarian lifestyle. But our time is different. Our modern living environment is crowded and noisy while tranquility and the sounds of nature are hard to come by. Only on weekends are people free to escape from the cities, but to their dismay all waterfronts and beautiful woods are packed with people. Everywhere one goes there are lots of people and noises; nowhere can you find a peaceful place for meditation. When one finally arrives at home after putting up with traffic jams and foul air, one is again greeted by doorbells and phones ringing, neighbors' barking dogs, vendors shouting through megaphones, honking cars, roaring scooters, sirens of fire trucks, ambulances, and police cars...and on top of that, one has to entertain visitors or pay visits back to them. When finally one can sit down on the meditation mat, the phone may go off again.

In such a stressful and chaotic environment, one is fortunate if one can spare an hour every day for meditation. Nobody can afford the luxury of four, five, or even eight, nine hours of daily meditation. Without adequate and uninterrupted time for practice as well as a quiet environment, how is it possible to cultivate the Dharma-door for perfect mastery through the ear faculty? For today's Chan and Pure Land practitioners, an ideal practice method is one that can be carried out during any kind of activity, regardless whether one is in stillness or in a state of physical activity. This method of signless mindfulness of Buddha fits the bill perfectly. More importantly, since it works directly with the mental faculty, its mastery equips one with the ability to maintain mindfulness of Buddha under any circumstances. Even when one is constantly moving around amidst all kinds of sensory stimulation, the pure thought of Buddha can be held without disruption. This ability is what the Chan masters meant by "riding the sounds and capping the forms (騎聲蓋色)." This level of in-motion meditative concentration allows one to continue the cultivation of the Great Śūraṅgama Samādhi, take rebirth in the pure lands of Buddhas, or practice Chan contemplation in daily life.

3. Thirdly, the scriptural passage on the Dharma-door of Buddha-mindfulness describes the recollection and mindfulness of Buddha with one's mind, and in the end, it says, "rein in all six sense faculties and abide in one pure continuous thought to enter samādhi." The words bear no reference to Buddha-mindfulness through recitation of Buddha's name whatsoever. For example:

> If sentient beings recollect and are mindful of Buddha, certainly they will see the Buddha now or in the future. They will never be far from the Buddha....On the causal ground, I entered the acquiescence to the non-arising with a mind that yearns for the Buddha.

All these words characterize a practice method directly within the mind. The first quote above speaks about yearning for the Buddha instead of chanting the Buddha's name. In the second quote, Bodhisattva Mahāsthāmaprāpta states that he realized and entered the acquiescence to the non-arising of dharmas with a mind that yearns for the Buddha.

In practice, it is very difficult for a person who recites Buddha's name constantly in mind to enter a state of *samādhi*. Every single recitation of Buddha's name is comprised of several distracting thoughts and syllables. When one tries to keep Buddha's name going constantly in mind, it is impossible for him to enter samādhi. If the practitioner has minimal mental disturbances and right view, he will abandon Buddha's name when discursive thoughts no longer emerge. He will then maintain or abide in the one pure thought of

Buddha without being attached to it, and his mind will gradually enter samādhi. Still, compared to the mindfulness of Buddha, this cultivation process is more roundabout and less direct.

As for people who choose to chant Buddha's name aloud with a focused mind in a sitting posture, they will have even more difficulty entering a state of samādhi. Practitioners with minimal mental disturbances may be able to enter samādhi, that is, a state of mental absorption, while chanting the name of Buddha continuously, provided they are able to detach from the mindfulness itself when discursive thoughts stop arising in mind and that they can let the oral chanting continue at a moderate pace while single-mindedly holding the thought of Buddha in mind without clinging to it. However, compared to the previous method, this course of practice demands even higher degree of meditative concentration and therefore is even harder to achieve. Thus, it is much easier and straightforward to enter samādhi by recollecting and being mindful of Buddha, which is a method that can be quickly mastered without harming the balance of your internal energy.

The mindfulness of Buddha works directly with the attention of the mind, that is, the mental faculty, rather than going through the tongue or the ear faculty first. "I would select no other method than this: rein in all six sense faculties and abide in one continuous pure thought to enter *samādhi*. This is the foremost method." As the words of Bodhisattva Mahāsthāmaprāpta indicate, this Dharma-door of Buddha-mindfulness does not rely on any signs, but is a Pure Land method based on samādhi cultivation. Practitioners have to abandon image, language, and name to directly yearn for Buddha with the mind. Only when this pure thought of Buddha is held without interruption can one's practice be considered "reining in all six sense faculties and abiding in one continuous pure thought." If any other thought or Buddha's name crops up in the mind, then one is no longer "abiding in one continuous pure thought." By maintaining this continuous and uninterrupted pure thought of Buddha, one can eventually enter samādhi. Those with the sharpest faculty can even attain the state of ultimate liberation by realizing the emptiness of the five aggregates, which is the ultimate, Mind-Only pure land. Such is the essence of Bodhisattva Mahāsthāmaprāpta's Dharma-door for perfect mastery through Buddha-mindfulness.

In conclusion, Bodhisattva Mahāsthāmaprāpta's Dharma-door is a method of signless mindfulness of Buddha and a way to cultivate the Pure Land through samādhi training. Please do not reject this method with the supposition that most Buddhist teachers regard and teach Bodhisattva Mahāsthāmaprāpta's Dharma-door for perfect mastery through Buddha-mindfulness as a method based on the recitation of Buddha's name only. Many Buddhist teachers use the name recitation method as an introductory expedient to ease their students into this method. I am convinced that Buddhist teachers will proceed to teach the profound principles underlying the practice of signless mindfulness when they see that conditions are ripe to do so, so that they can perfect their enormous merits in propagating the incredible Dharma-door for perfect mastery through Buddha-mindfulness.

3.4 Fundamental Knowledge, Part 2: Buddhist Practitioners Should Leave Behind the Three Poisons and Abandon the Mind's Habitual Tendencies of Clinging and Grasping, Perceiving and Observing

Chan Master Daoxin (道信禪師; 580–651), the fourth patriarch of the Chan school, says:

> Expel the mind of three poisons, the clinging and grasping mind, and the perceiving and observing mind. Bear the Buddha in mind continuously in every moment. Suddenly the mind will become lucid and tranquil without any objects to attend to. The *Mahāprajñāpāramitā Sūtra* says: "The one without thought is the one that bears the Buddha in mind." What is the one without thought? The mind that bears the Buddha is called the one without thought.... Why so? Because consciousness is without form, and Buddha is without form or appearance.[29]

---

[29] *Record of the Masters and Disciples of the Lankāvatāra Sūtra* 楞伽

These words of Chan Master Daoxin are meant to eliminate or reduce practitioners' attachment to physical forms, names, sounds, and deluded thoughts.

Ordinary people cannot realize the Buddha-nature mainly because they are obstructed by the "three poisons": greed, aversion, and ignorance. They therefore crave visual, auditory, olfactory, gustatory, and tactile stimuli, or in a more worldly sense, money, sex, fame, food and sleep. They often fail to defer to their superiors or respect their subordinates, and fly into a rage when things don't go their way. When they lack adequate wealth, power, or physical strength to compete with their opponents, they resort to backstabbing and secret retaliation. If they have an edge over others, they openly take advantage of others' weakness. All such physical, verbal and mental acts of greed and aversion stem from ignorance. Consequently, people are not able to see the reality of the dharma-realm, but regard the material world as real and develop attachment to it. Unable to see the absolute emptiness and sublime existence of the self-nature, they cling to the illusory five aggregates as their real self and engage in actions that produce all kinds of karma. The better sort of people seek rebirth in the heavenly realms by doing virtuous deeds; the average sort pursue the rewards of fame and fortune in this life through wholesome acts; and the lowest sort are hypocrites who prey upon others using brute force or cunning schemes. Thus, their minds are constantly grasping at something and their every thought is tainted with greed, aversion, and ignorance.

師資記. CBETA, T85, no. 2837, p1287a9-14: 摒除三毒心、攀緣心、覺觀心。念佛心心相續，忽然澄寂，更無所緣念。大品經云：'無所念者，是名念佛'，何等名無所念？即念佛心，名無所念。...所以者何？識無形、佛無形、佛無相貌。

If one has realized the self-nature and does not regress from this realization, one should be able to observe the inherent Buddha-nature characterized by absolute emptiness and sublime existence. Upon this realization, the feeling of the body, mind, and physical world as being real abruptly disappears. As a result, one's attachment to them will not arise and the three poisons naturally lose their power, enabling one to abandon unwholesome acts.

Being an ordinary, unenlightened person, one should contemplate the impermanence of the body, mind, and physical world, and reflect on the fact that these transient phenomena are brought about by conjunction of causes and conditions and hence will eventually disintegrate and perish. If a practitioner constantly reflects upon impermanence in relation to everyday events and deepens this reflection during sitting meditation, he can reduce his attachment to the physical world, body and mind, as well as family, fame and wealth. The power of the three poisons will lessen as a result, which will in turn weaken the mind's predisposition to grasp at sensory objects. It will then be much easier for the practitioner to rest his mind in the correct mindfulness of Buddha.

In this impure world of five turbidities, it is extremely rare to find a person who seeks liberation from cyclical birth-and-death within the three realms by way of the various Buddhist Dharma-doors, such as samādhi cultivation, Chan contemplation, and Pure Land practices, and at the same time dedicate the merits of his cultivation toward all sentient beings and assist them to achieve the same goal. Unfortunately, among the many practitioners, only a few are able to master and succeed in their practice. Lacking correct views while keen on receiving empathetic connections from Buddha, most practitioners tend to constantly perceive and observe external states during their practice. This tenacious habit of the mind hinders practitioners of Buddha-mindfulness, Chan contemplation, as well as meditative concentration from reaching undisturbed one-pointed focus.

In the following paragraphs, I will give a brief explanation, from a basic to a deeper level, of the mind's habitual tendencies of perceiving and observing, so that practitioners can establish correct understanding in this subject and apply it in their practice. I urge all practitioners to read and reflect upon these paragraphs carefully.

Hoping to receive extraordinary signs or visions, some Pure Land practitioners constantly watch out for unusual signs during their practice. Whenever they detect any such signs, such as special light, sounds, fragrances, or mental and physical serenity, their minds will cling to them and begin to fluctuate. Because of this, it is extremely difficult for them to achieve single-minded concentration. Occasionally, some practitioners are able to chant Buddha's name to a point where no distracting thoughts arise in their minds. While they feel the urge to drop the Buddha's name and settle in a state of mental absorption upon reaching this stage, they hesitate to do so due to a deficient understanding of samādhi cultivation. The vexing indecision of whether to continue with or leave behind the Buddha's name keeps them from reaching a single-minded focus.

At this juncture, a practitioner with adequate knowledge and wholesome roots will abandon Buddha's name and move on to dwell in the state of signless mindfulness of Buddha. If he does not rejoice in this achievement but keeps his mind from stirring even when he experiences a connection with Buddha (in the form of a ray of light, the smell of a fragrance, or the experience of mental and physical serenity for instance), and if he can consistently achieve this day in and day out, he will eventually be able to hold a signless thought of Buddha whether he is in physical motion or in stillness. Over time, the mastery of signless Buddha-mindfulness would enable him to see the "first sudden instance of awareness [of an object]"[30] and gradually attain the various kinds of Buddha-Mindfulness Samādhi. All these attainments are preconditioned on the ability to abandon the coarse form of perception and observation.

In a nutshell, the three poisons, and the mind's habitual tendencies of clinging and grasping, perceiving and observing are pitfalls that all practitioners of Buddha-mindfulness should stay away from.

The three poisons of greed, aversion and ignorance are harmful to samādhi practitioners in the exact same ways as described above. As for Chan practitioners, a small number of them consider themselves as having a superior capacity and scorn practitioners of the Pure Land tradition. They think that Pure Land practitioners have inferior capacity and seek rebirth in the Buddhas' pure lands because of insufficient faith and Dharma knowledge. The truth is there are many Pure Land practitioners with a sharp capacity, who can practice mindfulness of Buddha to the point where their minds are rid of all thoughts, including the thought of Buddha, and settle into a firm and stable state of mental absorption.

A small percentage of Chan practitioners not only despise Pure Land practitioners but also feel superior to Chan practitioners of their own groups or other practice centers. They are filled with conceit and are unwilling to listen to others' ideas or experiences. Apart from the three poisons, these people are also plagued by arrogance, a mentality that aggravates aversion and malice. Arrogance is

---

[30] Skt. *Aupanipātika*; Chi. 介爾初心

66

extremely detrimental to the cultivation of Chan and meditative concentration. Unless it is eliminated, one will constantly compare oneself with others and one's chance of achieving mental focus or seeing Buddha-nature is next to impossible—like an ordinary person wishing he could walk on the moon.

The conscious mind's tendencies toward clinging and grasping hinder the cultivation of meditative concentration for both novice and seasoned practitioners. The untrained mind of beginners tend to be easily distracted by sounds during their practice of mindfulness. When they finally become aware of their scattered mind, it has already wandered through a long train of thoughts. They still have a long way to go before they can achieve mental absorption. On the other hand, experienced practitioners tend to preoccupy themselves with thoughts about the Buddha Dharma or the feeling of serenity and composure during their practice. Their minds cannot stay focused but constantly give in to the tenacious tendencies of clinging and grasping. They too have difficulty achieving mental focus.

There are different ways to rid the mind of its tendencies to cling to sensory objects whether one cultivate meditative concentration in stillness or in movement. The practice of signless Buddha-mindfulness introduced in this book is a method that can be practiced whether one is in stillness or in motion, and it can be picked up fairly easily by way of two introductory expedient means: prostration to Buddha with signless mindfulness and recitation of Buddha's name.

Moreover, the mind's tenacious tendencies of perceiving and observing not only afflict practitioners of meditative concentration but also Chan practitioners in the following ways:

1. Breath-counting is a common technique used by samādhi practitioners to focus the mind in a continuous state. In the beginning, when the mind is scattered, one counts each breath in a one-to-ten cycle repeatedly. Once the mind is trained to stop clinging and grasping, one can switch from breath-counting to simply keeping one's attention on the breathing, until the mind is unified with the breathing. By this time, the coarse form of perception and observation will have been eliminated. A knowledgeable practitioner would then use a subtler form of perception and observation to discerningly select one of the many favorable mental states that arises from the unified mind and settle in it. If he is able to dwell in this state over an extended period of time, his mind will become more focused and discerning. Thereupon, he should gradually abandon the subtler form of perception and observation in order to enter the state of access concentration.31 Once he is able to enter the access concentration and becomes proficient in it, he can attain the first concentration (dhyāna)32 with clear perception and observation when he has overcome the dispositional hindrances.33 The first concentration comes with the

---

31 Skt. *upacārasamādhi*; Chi.未到地定.

32 The Sanskrit word *dhyāna* denotes meditative absorption and the practices that aimed at focusing the mind in one-pointedness to the exclusion of all other objects. The first concentration 初禪 is one of the four levels of mental absorptions that correspond to the form realm. The four formless absorptions are even higher level of meditative absorption that correspond to the states of the formless realm.

33 Dispositional hindrances 性障: refers to hindrances constituted by

meritorious qualities of pleasurable physical touch, known as the bliss of one-pointed perception and observation.

However, in the steps described above, if the practitioner is still attached to the mind's perceiving and observing tendencies and is unwilling to abandon them in the later stage of the practice, he would not be able to reach the stage of access concentration. Without sufficient power of meditative concentration to enter the state of access concentration, he can never attain the first concentration, let alone the second, third, or the fourth concentration.

In brief, to achieve a deeper level of concentration, one ought to first abandon the rough and coarse form of perception and observation in order to sustain mental attention upon one single object. Then, one should arouse the subtler form of perception and observation in order to abide in a finer and subtler mental state. After one is able to abide in the finer and subtler mental state with ease and competence, one should again abandon this subtler state so as to enter access concentration and eventually the first concentration. The same techniques and process apply to the cultivation of the second, third, and fourth concentrations, as well as the four formless absorptions.

A practitioner with a sound understanding of the perceiving and observing tendencies of the mind can enter samādhi and attain all levels of meditative

---

the nature of an unenlightened person.

absorptions by moving from the coarse to the subtle form of perception and observation, and eventually even abandoning the subtle form altogether. On top of that, he knows how to cast off the illusive states generated by the six forms of consciousness and keep his mind unstirred. Conversely, if a practitioner cannot overcome the perceiving and observing tendencies of the mind, he will be deluded by the various illusive states brought forth by the six forms of consciousness. This would give demons the opportunity to lead him astray from his practice. As a result, he may falsely proclaim that he has realized some noble states or the various levels of meditative absorptions and consequently fall into evil destinies despite efforts for higher existence. Or, he may attract the company of pestering ghosts and spirits and will be unable to focus his mind or enter deeper into the profound states of Buddha.

2. The abandoning of perception and observation is even more important for Chan practitioners. If perception and observation persist interminably, practitioners will not be able to develop an integrated and pervasive level of meditative concentration. As a result, the "sense of doubt" either fails to arise or is simply not strong enough, and it would be impossible for one to enter the stage of "seeing the mountain as not being mountain, viewing the water as not being water," (Note 7) let alone breaking through the mass of doubt to achieve awakening to the Buddha-nature. Wuyi Yuanlai (無異元來; 1575–ca. 1630) of Mt. Bo was a prominent Chan master of the late Ming Dynasty and the author of *General Discourse on the*

Core Essence and its Teachings.[34] He was an eminent monk who demonstrated both doctrinal and instructional excellence. His work *Monk Boshan's Exhortations for Chan Contemplation*[35] has been handed down for generations and has guided Chan practitioners in honing their skills. In his book, Wuyi Yuanlai amply illustrates the faults of the perceiving and observing tendencies of the mind. He also exhorted that "one should not let the mind await awakening." Should a Chan practitioner passively wait for awakening when the sense of doubt arises, he will not be able to enter the stage of "seeing the mountain as not being mountain." Without this level of meditative concentration, it is exceedingly difficult for a person to realize the True Mind and see the Buddha-nature on his own. He would have to rely on the guidance and goading of a virtuous and knowledgeable mentor skilled in both doctrinal understanding and instructional expedients. However, such a mentor is extremely hard to come by.

Additionally, Master Wuyi Yuanlai also stresses the followings:

> During practice, focus only on the unbroken sense of doubt and keep no other thoughts....The presence of any other thoughts, no matter how fine and subtle, will hurt your wisdom-life....What I mean by "other thoughts" include not only thoughts of mundane affairs, but also any

---

[34] *Zongjiao tongshuo* 宗教通說
[35] *Boshan heshang canchan jingyu* 博山和尚參禪警語 (CBETA, X63, no 1257)

wholesome, Dharma-related issues apart from the investigation of the mind. In fact, not only matters of the Buddha Dharma, any apprehending and abandoning, clinging and relinquishing of the mind is considered "other thoughts."[36]

Why is this so vital in Chan contemplation? Precisely because the tenacious tendencies of constant perception and observation is a serious impediment to Chan contemplation. It causes one to frequently drop the *huatou*. As a result, the sense of doubt will fail to arise, making it impossible for one to even contemplate Chan.

For the same reasons stated above, Pure Land practitioners should also eliminate the three poisons, the mind's habitual tendencies of clinging and grasping, perceiving and observing in order to maintain unbroken mindfulness. The objective is to bring the mind to undisturbed one-pointed focus, wherein it is lucid and quiescent, attends to and grasps at nothing—be it the image of name of Buddha, the sound of Buddha's name, or even the thought of mindfulness itself.

In his writing, Chan Master Daoxin cites the *Mahāprajñāpāramitā Sūtra* to explain this point: "'The one without thought is the one that bears the Buddha in mind.' What is the one without thought? The mind that bears the

---

[36] *Boshan heshang canchan jingyu* 博山和尚參禪警語.CBETA, X63, no. 1257, 758a23-758b3: 做工夫。著不得一絲毫別念。... 若有絲毫別念....此傷乎慧命...余云別念。非但世間法。除究心之外。佛法中一切好事悉名別念。又豈但佛法中事。於心體上取之捨之。執之化之。悉別念矣。

Buddha is called the one without thought." In other words, one should practice with the ultimate truth as the fundamental basis no matter which Dharma-door one goes with. Then one will not cling to a form-aggregate self, nor a sensation-, perception-, formation-, or consciousness-aggregate self, and the three poisons, and the clinging and grasping, perceiving, and observing tendencies of the mind will not come forth. Attachment to all mundane and supramundane phenomena will cease and one will reach a state in which one's mind does not even attend to a single object. Thereupon, one is considered to be the "one without thought." The pure, lucid, and tranquil mind that attends to no object is the mind of true Buddha-mindfulness, the state of "one-pointed absorption within principle," and the state of "Buddha-mindfulness in Ultimate Reality." In his book, *A Discourse on Buddha-Mindfulness Samādhi in the Avataṃsakasūtra*, [37] lay Buddhist Peng Erlin (彭二林) describes such a state in these words:

> Knowing that all Buddhas and one's own mind are like dreams; that all Buddhas are like images and reflections, with one's own mind being the water; that the forms of all Buddhas and one's own mind are both illusive; that all Buddhas and one's own mind are like echoes. In this way I know and am mindful of all Buddhas, as all Buddhas I see originate from my true mind.[38]

---

[37] *Huayan nianfo sanmei lun* 華嚴念佛三昧論
[38] *Huayan nianfo sanmei lun* 華嚴念佛三昧論. CETA, X58, no. 1030, 714b4: 知一切佛及以我心。悉皆如夢。知一切佛猶如影像。自心如水。知一切佛所有色相。及以自心。悉皆如幻。知一切佛及以己心。悉皆如響。我如是知。如是憶念。所見諸佛皆由自心。

A person who reaches the state of "one-pointed absorption within principle" must have cultivated Chan and Pure Land concurrently and passed through the stage of contemplative Buddha-mindfulness. He has directly perceived the original face of the one "who is bearing the Buddha in mind?" and will not regress from this realization. He can see his intrinsic Buddha-nature at all times with the mind's eye and will never regress from this direct perception no matter how much time has passed. This accomplishment is not only beyond the reach of most Pure Land practitioners but also rarely achieved by Chan practitioners. As Chan Master Huangbo Xiyun (黃蘗希運; d. 850) said: "Out of tens of thousands of practitioners, only three, or maybe five, can pass through this gate." [39] Therefore, there is no reason for Chan practitioners to scorn Pure Land practitioners or underestimate this Dharma-door of signless Buddha-mindfulness.

Signless Buddha-mindfulness can actually be practiced at many different levels ranging from simple to profound. At the introductory level, it enables one to attain "one-pointed absorption within phenomena," a state not at all easy to reach for an average Chan practitioner. At the advanced levels, it not only leads to the realization of "one-pointed absorption within principle" but also the attainment of ultimate liberation, even to the stages of Virtual Enlightenment and Sublime Enlightenment.

Bodhisattva Mahāsthāmaprāpta's discourse on the Dharma-door for perfect mastery through Buddha-mindfulness starts right off with this statement: "Dharma-prince Mahāsthāmaprāpta, together with fifty-two fellow bodhisattvas, arose from their seats and prostrated at the

---

[39] *Guzunsu yulu juan disan* 古尊宿語錄卷第三: CBETA, X68, no. 1315, p23105: 此門中千人萬人。祇得三箇五箇。

Buddha's feet…." In the grand assembly of the *Śūraṅgama Sūtra*, there were countless bodhisattvas who had been practicing Bodhisattva Mahāsthāmaprāpta's Dharma-door for perfect mastery through Buddha-mindfulness. These bodhisattvas were represented by the fifty-two bodhisattvas who accompanied Bodhisattva Mahāsthāmaprāpta to prostrate at the Buddha's feet before he explained this Dharma-door. Why was there fifty-two and not some other number of bodhisattvas accompanying Bodhisattva Mahāsthāmaprāpta? Because the number fifty-two carries a profound meaning with it. It alludes to the fact that this Dharma-door can be practiced at various levels from simple to profound and that it can be learned by practitioners of all capacities—including unenlightened novice bodhisattvas at the beginner's level, bodhisattvas at the ten Faith stages as well as the three stages of worthiness,[40] bodhisattvas at the noble stages (the first to tenth Ground), and even bodhisattvas at the stages of Virtual Enlightenment and Sublime Enlightenment, who are about to attain Buddhahood. The fact that innumerable bodhisattvas cultivate this Dharma-door for perfect mastery through Buddha-mindfulness underscores its incredible efficacy and marvelousness.

The steps detailed in this book can help a person who initially practices sign-dependent mindfulness of Buddha with a scattered mind to reach the stage of "one-pointed absorption within phenomena," that is, proficient signless mindfulness of Buddha. Insomuch that this level of Buddha-mindfulness equips one with the power of in-motion meditative concentration, it affords one the ability to hold

---

[40] Three stages of worthiness 三賢位: the ten stages of Abiding, Practice, and Dedication (十住、十行、十迴向) of the bodhisattva path.

in mind a pure and signless thought of Buddha continuously at any time during one's frantic modern life. When one has acquired this level of in-motion concentration, one can easily achieve the same level of mental focus during sitting meditation as well. As for whether a practitioner can advance to the stage of "one-pointed absorption within principle," it depends on a number of factors: 1) merits and wisdom one has accumulated over the previous lifetimes; 2) one's causes and conditions as well as karmic retributions; and 3) whether one can overcome circumstantial hindrances and eradicate dispositional hindrances to carry on one's practice with due diligence.

Practitioners who have gained preliminary success in the Dharma-door for perfect mastery through Buddha-mindfulness (the equivalent to achieving signless mindfulness of Buddha to the point of "one-pointed absorption within phenomena"), when they pass away from the current world in the future, they can take rebirth as they wish in either the Realm of True Reward and Adornment or the Realm of Expedients and Remainders in the Pure Land of Ultimate Bliss. This, however, excludes those who are still attached to their possessions in the mundane world and unwilling to forgo their family, riches, and careers, or those who fail to accord with the specific vows of Buddhas (Note 8). Those with sufficient wholesome roots, stocks of merit, as well as expedient skills can take rebirth in any Buddha's pure land if they deepen their cultivation to reach the stage of "one-pointed absorption within principle." They could as well choose to dwell in the Mind-Only Pure Land if they do not wish to be reborn in a Buddha's pure land. Moreover, practitioners who have achieved "one-pointed absorption within phenomena" by having mastered signless Buddha-mindfulness can certainly take rebirth in the Pure Land of Ultimate Bliss. Alternatively, they can also elevate their level and grade of rebirth in the Pure Land by furthering their practices. This will allow them to return sooner to the Sahā world[41] to liberate and deliver sentient beings from sufferings.

Chan practitioners not keen on entering deeper into the Dharma-door for perfect mastery through Buddha-mindfulness can use this practice as stepping stone in their cultivation and discard it after use—although this method is incredibly valuable. They can take advantage of this method as if it is a boat that ferries one across the river and becomes useless once the shore is reached. Once a Chan practitioner has acquired the ability of in-motion meditative concentration through this Dharma-door, he would be able to guard the *huatou* or contemplate the *gong'an*. He can then contemplate Chan competently and effectively. A committed Chan practitioner who has yet to develop the ability to guard the *huatou* should not give up on this effective and ingenious training of in-motion meditative concentration simply because of personal dislike of its entrance expedients—prostration to Buddha and recitation of Buddha's name. He can always return to Chan cultivation once he has acquired the power of in-motion meditative concentration, which is highly conducive to Chan cultivation. So why not take advantage of it? Last but not least, this Dharma-door is best practiced when one is in physical motion. All it takes is ten to twenty minutes of prostration to Buddha each morning and evening. Nothing can be more convenient for busy Buddhist learners of the modern world.

Before trying out this seemingly ordinary Dharma-door and its practice methods detailed in chapter 4, please think

---

[41] Sahāloka 娑婆世界, literally the "world of endurance" in Sanskrit, is the world system we inhabit and a Buddha-field overseen by Buddha Śākyamuni.

through what I have explained thus far with respect to its foundational knowledge and understand its core concepts. The mastery of signless mindfulness of Buddha is guaranteed as long as one follows the methods and steps with due diligence. This Dharma-door can not only help secure one's rebirth in the pure land, but also provide one with the specific skill essential for Chan contemplation or contemplative Buddha-mindfulness. What greater joy is there!

Chapter 4

Cultivation Method and Sequence of Signless Buddha-Mindfulness

4.1 The Three Refuges and the Three Blessed Pure Deeds

If a practitioner (Note 9) had not become a Buddhist disciple by taking the threefold refuge, he should contact a traditional, orthodox Buddhist monastery nearby concerning the process. The formal ceremony is not complicated at all. The key is that the ceremony has to be conducted in front of a Buddha statue in a monastery and witnessed by a Buddhist monk or nun who will confer the three refuges: refuge in Buddha, in the Dharma taught by Buddha, and in the Sangha comprised of saints and sages and also those enlightened bodhisattvas or ordinary monks who can uphold the Buddha Dharma. As part of the ceremony, one has to make the Four Vast Vows:

Countless are sentient beings, I vow to liberate them;
Endless are vexations, I vow to eradicate them;
Innumerable are the Dharma-doors, I vow to master them;
Unsurpassable is the Buddha's Way, I vow to attain it.

These wishes are shared among all Buddhas. By taking this threefold refuge, one becomes an official disciple of the Three Jewels: Buddha, Dharma, and Sangha. This is the prerequisite condition for practicing the Dharma-door of Buddha-mindfulness. If one's mind is not determined enough to take the threefold refuge, it is absolutely impossible to attain Buddha-Mindfulness Samādhi through the cultivation of the Dharma-door for perfect mastery of Buddha-mindfulness.

Before taking the threefold refuge, one should learn the proper way to prostrate to Buddha from a member of the Sangha. The correct way to prostrate to Buddha requires five points of the body touching the ground in order to show admiration and reverence toward the World-Honored One, the Supreme Teacher of all humans and celestial beings. Deep admiration and respect give rise to deep faith. Also, relying on Buddhas' virtues and vow powers, one can quickly master this Dharma-door. As for the precise movements of prostration, please consult monasteries or fellow Buddhists disciples. I will not go over them here.

The *Sūtra on the Contemplation of Buddha Amitāyus* states:

> I now extensively explain the various metaphors for you, and also for all those ordinary people in future lifetimes who seek the cultivation of the pure deeds to be born into the Western Pure Land of Ultimate Bliss. Those who seek rebirth in that Buddha land should cultivate the three blessed pure deeds. They should make offerings with filial piety to their parents and serve their

teachers with respect. They should be kind-hearted and refrain from killing. They should cultivate the ten wholesome deeds. Secondly, they should receive and uphold the three refuges and fulfill all moral precepts without violating the majestic and dignified deportment. Lastly, they should bring forth the bodhi mind and have deep faith in causality. They should study and recite the Mahāyāna doctrines and encourage others to do likewise.[42]

Accordingly, all ordinary people who seek to cultivate pure deeds and gain rebirth in Buddhas' pure land should fulfill the three blessed pure deeds described above. The practice of signless Buddha-mindfulness, a Dharma-door that can be practiced across the Pure Land, Chan, and esoteric schools, also needs the three blessed pure deeds as a foundation.

If one has a hard time picking up this Dharma-door, most likely it is because one has not cultivated the three pure blessed deeds in the current or former lives. One should fulfill these supporting conditions as soon as possible. If one still has questions about their cultivation, please consult a virtuous and knowledgeable Buddhist mentor for a thorough explanation.

Furthermore, a vegetarian diet is most conducive to the practice of signless mindfulness of Buddha. If one cannot

---

[42] *Sūtra on the Contemplation of Buddha Amitayus* 佛說觀無量壽佛經. CBETA, T12, no. 365, 341c4: 我今為汝廣說眾譬，亦令未來世一切凡夫欲修淨業者，得生西方極樂國土。欲生彼國者，當修三福：一者、孝養父母，奉事師長，慈心不殺，修十善業。二者、受持三歸，具足眾戒，不犯威儀。三者、發菩提心，深信因果，讀誦大乘，勸進行者。如此三事名為淨業。

follow a strict vegetarian diet, one can compromise by eating just the vegetables in non-vegetarian dishes. However, the five pungent herbs—chives, garlic (including garlic shoots), leek, onion and asafetida—should not be consumed. Also, smoking and drinking of alcohol should be absolutely avoided. If alcohol is consumed as medication, it should be taken strictly in accordance to the amount and frequency prescribed and not for pleasure purposes. These rules are meant to enhance the supporting conditions and reduce hindrances for one's practice, so please pay close attention to their observance.

4.2 Key to the Buddha Prostration Practice

A practitioner should start practicing prostration for ten to twenty minutes at home every morning and evening after taking the three refuges proceedings and becoming proficient with the proper movements of Buddha prostration. It is not necessary to prostrate in front of a statue or an image of Buddha, or even in a formal worshiping area. Any clean and quiet places, such as a den, a living room, or even a tidy workroom or bedroom would suffice. It certainly would be better if one has a formal worshiping area at home with a statue or an image of Buddha, in which case one can practice prostration for ten to twenty minutes after offering incense to Buddha every morning and evening.

Signless Buddha Prostration Practice: Buddha prostrations should be done in very slow motion. Staying mentally focused is more important than the number of prostrations you perform. During prostration, do not recite Buddha's name but concentrate on every movement your body makes and how your body feels. If you notice your mind starts drifting away, simply bring it back to focus on the prostration movements of your body. Focus single-mindedly on your Buddha prostration movements no matter what earth-shaking events are going on around you.

Do not prostrate too fast as your pulse and heartbeat will accelerate. This will make it difficult for you to maintain concentration and your mind would become easily distracted. The prostration has to be carried out as slowly as possible and the pace should not exceed two prostrations per minute at a maximum. The most suitable pace for beginners is about forty-five seconds to one minute per prostration. When prostrating, your mind is supposed to be completely absorbed in your movements without paying attention to anything else. Usually, after two days of practice and adjustment you will become accustomed to this kind of slow-motion Buddha prostration, which is essential to your practice.

4.3 Prostration to Buddha with Signless Mindfulness: An Expedient Method to Cultivate the Dharma-Door for Perfect Mastery through Buddha-Mindfulness

Prostration to Buddha with signless mindfulness: Before you start, choose one specific Buddha or bodhisattva to be the object of your prostration practice. While the most common choices are Buddha Śākyamuni, Buddha Amitābha, Buddha Bhaiṣajyaguru, Bodhisattva Avalokiteśvara, Bodhisattva Mahāsthāmaprāpta, Bodhisattva Mañjuśrī, Bodhisattva Samantabhadra, and Bodhisattva Kṣitigarbha, you are free to choose any other Buddhas or bodhisattvas you feel a strong connection with. Once you have made your choice, you should stick to it throughout your practice. You will be mindful of the same Buddha or bodhisattva all the way till you have mastered signless mindfulness of Buddha.

After you have selected a Buddha or bodhisattva, you may begin the prostration practice, during which you bear nothing but a pure thought of Buddha in mind. Usually, people recite Buddha's name once in mind before prostrating, and they repeat this routine three times in a row. But with this method, you should do away with the recitation completely while prostrating to the Buddha or bodhisattva of your choice. You should know clearly which Buddha or bodhisattva you are prostrating to, even though you do not recite His name verbally or mentally and do not hold any language, image or symbol of the Buddha or bodhisattva in your mind. The prostration must be carried out calmly and relaxingly in slow motion. Focus your mind and observe attentively whether you know with clarity which Buddha or bodhisattva you are prostrating to during each and every instant of your prostration. If Buddha's name or image arises in your mind, drop it right away and return to the pure thought of Buddha.

This prostration practice is an indispensable expedient method for cultivating the Dharma-door of signless Buddha-mindfulness as it is extremely difficult for a beginner to accomplish this Dharma-door without it. Therefore, one should not resist or reject this prostration practice; the meritorious qualities of Buddhas and bodhisattvas are so boundless that making prostrations to them with utmost sincerity brings you tremendous benefits. Besides, arrogance is the biggest obstruction for Buddhist learners. Prostrating to Buddhas and bodhisattvas, especially in public, is the most effective way to eliminate arrogance and is therefore conducive to one's Dharma cultivation.

Most people tend to cling to the image and name of Buddhas and bodhisattvas and cannot be mindful of Buddha without relying on them. In the previous chapter, I have quoted Chan Master Daoxin: " 'What is the one without thought?' The mind that bears the Buddha is called the one without thought.... Why so? Because consciousness is without form, and Buddha is without form or appearance." In other words, whatever is with appearance, sound, language, symbol, or even the word "Buddha" is not Buddha.

If language were Buddha, Buddha Śākyamuni should come out of our lips when we speak the words "Buddha Śākyamuni"; if sound were Buddha, Buddha Śākyamuni should appear when we say "Buddha Śākyamuni"; if written word were Buddha, Buddha Amitābha should appear when we write the words "Buddha Amitābha"; if the image were Buddha, all statues and images of Buddhas displayed in monasteries should turn into real Buddhas. A very famous *gong'an* in the Chan school goes like this: "Śākyamuni and Maitreya are still his servants, who is he?" Buddha Śākyamuni who manifested in our world over 2,500 years ago, and Buddha Maitreya (Note 10), who will appear in this world after millions of years, are merely *his* servants. Why don't you contemplate and find out exactly who *he* is? What this *gong'an* means is that the historical Buddha, Buddha Śākyamuni, who took birth in this world was only a response and emanation-body generated by His Dharma-body. So is Buddha Maitreya, the next Buddha to take birth in this human world.

Most Buddhist disciples know that Buddha has three bodies: the Dharma-body, the perfect reward-body, and the response and emanation-body. Buddha Śākyamuni who appeared in India 2,500 years ago was only a response and emanation-body. Since the timing and conditions were right for some people in this world to attain liberation, the Buddha took birth in our world as a prince in the palace of King Śuddhodana of Kapilavastu. He married and fathered a son, took excursions outside of the palace walls, and witnessed the sufferings of birth, aging, illness and death, which prompted him to leave the palace in the middle of night and became a monastic, pledging to liberate sentient beings from these sufferings. Having mastered all non-Buddhist teachings and practiced asceticism for six years, the Buddha realized that the attainment of Buddhahood does not lie in ascetic practices. He therefore bathed and accepted the offering of milk porridge. When he regained physical strength, He contemplated under the bodhi tree and attained perfect enlightenment of Buddhahood the moment he saw a bright star in the sky. Thereafter, he turned the wheel of Dharma, refuted the followers of other schools, liberated innumerable sentient beings, and eventually entered the great nirvana after manifesting aging and illness with his physical form. Dwelling in the neither-arising-nor-ceasing great nirvana, the Buddha is able to abide permanently in the mundane world and yet not abide anywhere. This is why sentient beings who have a karmic connection with the Buddha can still behold his visual manifestation. In other words, Buddha Śākyamuni was merely a response and emanation-body that was generated for the purpose of liberating sentient beings in this world who were ready to receive his teachings. Of course, for those people in whom the conditions were not yet ripe, he also planted seeds of future liberation. Once the Buddha finished what he came to this world for, he manifested the cessation of his earthly existence to remind sentient beings of impermanence.

Buddha's perfect reward-body is endowed with thirty-two majestic features and eighty associated good marks. It is shown to the hearers (*śrāvakas*) and bodhisattvas who reside in the Realm of Expedient with Remainder and the Realm of True Reward and Adornment so that they can learn directly from Buddha. The response and emanation-body and the reward-body are necessary for guiding and teaching sentient beings because the Dharma-body—the true "body" of Buddha—has neither form nor characteristics and is therefore invisible. Void of a physical body and its derivative features, or any language, sound, image and symbol, the Dharma-body cannot be shown or revealed but exhibits the unique characteristic called emptiness. Thus, this essence of Buddha cannot be named and the terms such as "Buddha" and "Dharma-body" are mere designations. This is why Chan Master Daoxin says, "The one without thought is the one that bears the Buddha in mind."

This truth can only be comprehended in depth when you have carried out considerable meditative contemplation after reaching the state of "one-pointed absorption within principle." While the realization of this truth is the cultivation objective of all Buddhist learners, it is not attainable by all. Yet, everyone who puts in a diligent effort can practice Buddha-mindfulness at the state of "one-pointed absorption within phenomena," that is, the signless mindfulness of Buddha. The long and repetitive explanations I have given above are for the purpose of helping practitioners to eliminate their attachment to names, images, and symbols of Buddha such that they can carry out signless mindfulness and this prostration practice with one-pointed concentration.

The recitation of Buddha's name and prostration to Buddha with signless mindfulness are effective entrance methods to the Dharma-door of signless Buddha-mindfulness. Recitation of Buddha's name is a method Buddha Śākyamuni presented for sentient beings of the Dharma-ending age who have weak faith. Relying on the power of Buddha Amitābha's great vows, people who chant His sacred name could be reborn in the Pure Land of Ultimate Bliss. However, this does not mean that everyone who practices recitation of Buddha's name will take rebirth in the pure land without exception. First, one must have strong faith and a firm resolve to take rebirth there, and be able to constantly chant Buddha's name orally or mentally during everyday life. In an emergency situation, the first thing that comes to mind should be Buddha Amitābha and one would automatically call out His name. Only with such solid skill can rebirth in the western pure land be ensured. Second, the sūtra stresses that to be born in the Buddha-land, one should not fall short of wholesome roots, merits, and right conditions. Only those who can recite Buddha's sacred name with single-minded concentration, constant mindfulness, and an undisturbed mind can achieve rebirth.

Regarding the nine grades of rebirth detailed in the *Sūtra on the Contemplation of Buddha Amitāyus*, rebirth in the top three grades of the highest level as well as the highest and middle grades of the middle level all require the fulfillment of specific conditions. Those who do not meet the requirements are usually born in the lowest grade of the middle level. They have to stay in the lotus palace for seven days before they can behold Bodhisattva Avalokiteśvara and Bodhisattva Mahāsthāmaprāpta, joyfully hear their Dharma instruction, and attain the fruition of stream-entry (the first fruition of the Path to Liberation). Then it would be another small eon before they attain arhatship (the fourth fruition of the Path to

Liberation) [note: One day in the Pure Land of Ultimate Bliss equals to one great eon in our world]. All practitioners should consider the incalculable length of time a person born in the lowest grade of the middle level has to spend in the lotus flower and the inconceivably long duration (one small eon in the Pure Land of Ultimate Bliss) it takes to advance from stream-entry to arhatship. In our Sahā world, even if you only cultivate the Dharma once every four lifetimes, your advancement will still be millions of times faster than those born in the lowest level of the middle grade in the Pure Land. All practitioners ought to weigh these factors.[43]

---

[43] For more details, please refer to the *Sūtra on the Descent of Maitreya* 彌勒下生經).

4.4 From Prostration to Buddha with Signless Mindfulness to Signless Buddha-Mindfulness: Ten Steps of Cultivation

STEP 1: Spend ten to twenty minutes every morning and evening to prostrate to Buddha according to the method detailed in section 4.3 of this chapter. Concentrate your mind on the one Buddha or bodhisattva of your choice and be mindful of him without chanting his name or forming any sound or word of him in mind. Despite the absence of words or images, you must know, with absolute clarity, which particular Buddha or bodhisattva you are holding in mind and making prostration to. Do not allow name or image to arise. There should only be one pure thought of yearning, as if you have been separated from your mother for decades and you are longing for her without her name or face appearing in mind. You should know clearly to which Buddha or bodhisattva you are prostrating and hold on to the pure thought of him unremittingly in every single instant. If you cannot grasp the idea of yearning, you can observe attentively whether the idea of "prostrating to

Buddha" is clear and distinct in your mind and whether you are aware of which Buddha or bodhisattva you are prostrating to.

As the accomplishment of signless Buddha-mindfulness hinges on this prostration practice, I urge all practitioners to mull over the underlying concepts I have laid down in previous chapters to understand this practice thoroughly. If you cannot understand it after thinking over it for a month or two, you should prostrate to a statue or a portrait of Buddha or bodhisattva (especially Buddha Śākyamuni, Bodhisattva Avalokiteśvara and Bodhisattva Mahāsthāmaprāpta) to repent your transgressions and ask for their blessings. You should also vow to take the Bodhisattva Precepts and commit to the bodhisattva's way to liberate countless living beings. Afterward, sit down and carefully read the previous paragraph and section 4.3 again. With conscientious practice and thorough reflection, you should be able to comprehend this practice method. If a statue or a portrait of Buddha or bodhisattva is unavailable, just prostrate to the empty space above. What matters is your sincerity, so please make sure you beseech Buddhas or bodhisattvas wholeheartedly rather than with a frivolous attitude.

Once you get a good grasp of signless mindfulness, practice prostration while lucidly holding in mind the Buddha or bodhisattva continuously, free of name or image. If the thought of Buddha is still vague and indistinct, try thinking of the Buddha instead. In the way that young lovers yearn for each other day and night when separated, contemplate that the formless and signless Dharma-body of the Buddha fills up the void and pervades everywhere, or think about his formless and signless Dharma-body abiding in your heart (not the physical organ) and mind, looking over and blessing you in each and every moment—such is the recollection and mindfulness for Buddha. The Chinese character 念 refers to "mindfulness" as in the term "Buddha-mindfulness" 念佛, which is written without the mouth radical 口. Otherwise, it would become 唸佛, the oral chanting of Buddha's name. You can connect with the Buddha if your chanting of his name is imbued with longing and yearning; otherwise, you will not mentally connect with the Buddha and take rebirth into his pure land regardless of how many years you practice.

If after much reading, reflecting and practicing, you still cannot grasp any of the idea of yearning, thinking, or recollecting, then while prostrating, try to focus on "watching" the idea of prostrating to Buddha, and see if you are clearly aware of which Buddha or bodhisattva you are prostrating to. Just watch this idea of prostrating without dropping it or letting the Buddha's name crop up in mind. Throughout each prostration, "guard" this thought, make sure it stays in mind and does not disappear. If it is not working, there is yet another method you can try.

Suppose you usually chant the name of Buddha Śākyamuni, then find a quiet spot to sit still and mentally recite "Buddha Śākyamuni" once (or the name of any Buddha or bodhisattva of your choice) while thinking of the Buddha. After the recitation is over, continue the thought of the Buddha and do not let it disappear. Keep this thought as long as possible until it finally fades away from your mind. The moment you realize that the thought is gone, start over again and recite "Buddha Śākyamuni" once in mind while thinking of him. Do not make another recitation but keep the thought in mind as long as you can. Repeat this process over again.

When you are proficient in this process, sit in front of a Buddha's statue or image in a quiet and undisturbed place in the morning. After you have settled down, chant silently in mind "Buddha Śākyamuni" (or any Buddha or bodhisattva of your choice) once while thinking of him. Meanwhile, introspect to see what is going on in your mind when the mental recitation is over, leaving only the thought of Buddha in your mind. Repeat the process again after you have examined your mental state, but this time, do not start from the mental recitation of Buddha's name. Instead, start from the point when the recitation of "Buddha Śākyamuni" has ended. The mental state after the recitation is finished is in essence the holding in mind of and yearning for Buddha, or what I call signless mindfulness of Buddha. Prostrate to the Buddha with this pure thought. This is the signless Buddha-mindfulness conjoined with prostrating.

At the beginning of this prostration practice, you need to exert a great deal of will power to suppress the emergence of Buddha's name or image in your mind. A little slip in concentration and they will crop up. Despite having to maintain total mental absorption, relax your body and do not tense up. After consistent daily practice, Buddha's name and image will gradually stop surfacing. Occasionally, the first syllable of Buddha's name may still come forth when you are not completely focused. The only way to drop the name altogether is to perform prostration with single-minded concentration each morning and evening persistently. If you have a relentless tendency to grasp at external states, instead of hearing the sounds of Buddha's name in your mind, the word "Buddha" often appears in your mind as an image. This is actually due to a deep-seated habitual tendency. To get rid of this tenacious tendency, reflect deeply that neither the name of a Buddha nor the word "Buddha" is the real Buddha. Some practitioners may even need to ponder over this thoroughly during sitting meditation.

It must be pointed out that your progress in this entry practice Dharma-door for perfect mastery through Buddha-mindfulness, that is, signless Buddha-mindfulness, depends entirely on whether you can grasp its essence and whether you can commit to your practice. Please pardon my tedious and repetitive explanations. Without thorough comprehension of signless Buddha-mindfulness through consistent daily prostration practice, it is impossible to accomplish this Dharma-door. Those who are of a superior capacity or already possess advanced proficiency in samādhi are exceptions to this rule, as they can pick up this method instantly and settle in the required mental state effortlessly.

So if you are just an average practitioner, please keep up the prostration practice for ten to twenty minutes every morning and evening. It will not only strengthen your power of meditative concentration but can also remove karmic hindrances. This practice is not time-consuming and therefore is compatible with today's busy lifestyle. On top of that, when one chanting of the Buddha's name is said to eliminate karmic transgressions as numerous as the grains of sand in the Ganges River, prostrating to Buddha with single-minded concentration can unquestionably clear away innumerable karmic wrongdoings.

Prostration to Buddha with signless mindfulness is a very effective way to build up the mind's power of meditative concentration. And since this power of meditative concentration is gained through an in-motion practice, by the time you have mastered signless mindfulness of Buddha, your body and mind will be able to maintain the mindfulness despite the presence of any sensory distractions.

A Supplementary Practice: If you have never practiced mindfulness of Buddha through name recitation and do not understand the concept of signless mindfulness, you need to first practice the recitation of Buddha's name alongside daily activities. Mentally recite Buddha's name and listen to your own recitation. This helps to reduce your mind's persistent tendency of grasping and absorb your mind from mental disturbances. You can make up a graceful melody with the name of the Buddha or the bodhisattva of your choice and sing the tune all the time in your mind while thinking of him. The tempo of this melody should not be brisk; the more elegant and solemn the better. And it should be sung as slow as possible. Also, only use one tune rather than a few different ones. Make sure that the one you prostrate to and the one you sing of are the same Buddha or bodhisattva. Do not practice prostration to Buddha Bhaiṣajyaguru with signless mindfulness and sing the name of Bodhisattva Avalokiteśvara. This is to ensure that your mind is attending to one Buddha or bodhisattva only. When you sing the sacred name of Buddha in mind, sing it slowly and steadily rather than trying to sing as many times as possible. Watch your mind and see if it is getting impatient or restless. Examine whether discursive thoughts are arising and whether the thought of Buddha is present or not. If you have practiced Buddha's name recitation before or have a clear understanding of the principle of Buddha-mindfulness, then you should focus on the practice of prostration to Buddha with signless mindfulness. You do not need the help of this supplementary expedient.

STEP 2: Practice prostration to Buddha with signless mindfulness for ten to twenty minutes every morning and evening consistently. Do not prostrate for two hours one day and skip for two days. Like rowing a boat, you must continue to row the oars or else your boat will drift off the set course or go back with the receding water. The length of prostration practice can be increased but not shortened. Other times, when you are not practicing prostrations, keep reciting Buddha's name in mind. After some time your scattered mind will gradually come under control. However, while discursive thoughts become fewer and fewer during prostrations and Buddha's name no longer arises, you will find that you are still easily distracted by sounds, such as phone rings, doorbells, people's voices, noises from TV and music, or the barking of dogs, and so forth. Whenever any sounds come within earshot, your mind immediately clings to them and generates an endless train of thoughts. Not until the current prostration is over and you are ready to start the next one do you remember to bring up the signless mindfulness of Buddha again. Do not feel frustrated as this is unavoidable for beginners. With determination and consistent daily prostration practice in conjunction with signless mindfulness of Buddha, complemented by mental recitation of Buddha's name (those who are already proficient in Buddha's name recitation should instead practice mindfulness of Buddha during the day), you will overcome this problem in time.

With consistent daily practice of prostration to Buddha in conjunction with signless mindfulness complemented by continuous Buddha-mindfulness or silent recitation of Buddha's name during the rest of the day, the grasping tendency of the mind will diminish until finally you are able to concentrate single-mindedly on prostrating to Buddha with signless mindfulness in spite of external sounds. This ability indicates the deepening of your level of meditative concentration and that five out of six of the sense faculties—the auditory, olfactory, gustatory, tactile, and mental faculties—have been brought under control. The visual faculty and the visual consciousness, however, are very hard to rein in. For example, you will often grasp at a strand of hair or some small objects on the floor during your practice. Every time you bow down you cannot help taking a glimpse of it, even though you know very well that you should focus your mind on the pure thought of Buddha. This kind of tenacious habit is in fact much subtler than other forms of grasping. Yet, it is very difficult to subdue as it is an entrenched habitual tendency of the visual faculty accumulated since time without a beginning. You are unable to overcome it given your current power of meditative concentration. The only way to cope with it is to close your eyes so you stop looking at your surroundings, and you can open your eyes once your meditative concentration has reached a more advanced level. When you are to close your eyes to overcome the eyes' persistent habit of clinging, you are ready to move on to Step 3.

STEP 3: Prostration to Buddha with Signless Mindfulness with Closed Eyes

Closing your eyes during prostration to Buddha with signless mindfulness helps you fight against the persistent habit of the eyes of wanting to see, making it much easier to keep the mind focused so that your power of meditative concentration can increase rapidly. Also, your thought of Buddha will be much clearer when your eyes are shut. Some people tend to feel dizzy when they prostrate with eyes closed. If you happen to experience this, find out the cause of your dizziness rather than giving up this stage of practice, for this is the most effective way to enhance your meditative concentration. Common causes of dizziness are listed as follows:

1. Disorientation: If you feel dizzy as a result of loss of direction, remind yourself in the following way before the prostration practice: "Buddha has neither physical body nor characteristic marks. His Dharma-body pervades every place. The Buddha is in my mind. The statue or image of him I am looking at is not Him, but merely a symbol and a device for me to rely on." Therefore, it is not necessary to make sure your body continues prostrating toward a particular direction. It does not matter if your body gradually changes direction or even if you end up with your back toward the Buddha statue. When the mental fixation on direction is removed, dizziness will go away when you prostrate with eyes closed.

2. Incorrect posture: As you bow and kneel down, make sure your head is not at a position lower than the rest of your body (this does not apply to people who do not experience dizziness). As well, when you finish prostration and lift up your body, keep your head slightly above the rest of the body. Bending your body and lowering your head cause blood to flow to your head, and dizziness results when blood rushes back to the body as you rise up all of a sudden. Another cause for dizziness is that your bottom is higher than the rest of your body when your head is touching the ground. In this case, lower your bottom and keep it close to

your legs to prevent too much blood from flowing to your head. If your pants are too tight or too stiff for you to bend down comfortably, put on looser clothing or stretchable casual wear with an elastic waistband, or use suspenders to hold your pants. Also, your nose should touch the ground when your head does. This makes sure that you do not touch the ground with just the top of your head.

3. Overweight: People who are overweight should use a cushion about 20 cm thick. During prostration, keep your feet and knees on the ground and rest your head, palms and elbows on the cushion. This will relieve dizziness by preventing blood from rushing to your head.

Once you do not feel dizzy when you prostrate with your eyes closed, you can continue with your practice. Through consistent and focused daily practice, you will stop grasping at external states and make much speedier progress than in the previous stages. Rarely will Buddha's name emerge in your mind.

STEP 4: Avoid Regulating Your Breath
After overcoming the difficulties of the previous stage, you will find that while your mind no longer grasps at any sensory object, your breathing is somewhat difficult or you feel a lump in your throat. Our mind craves the apprehension of some kind of objects. When all the five

sense faculties (visual, auditory, olfactory, gustatory, and mental) are restrained from their usual habits, the mind then grabs hold of the body's breathing process. You may start to unconsciously regulate your breathing during prostration. You do not notice this at first and it usually takes a few weeks before you become aware of the discomfort in your throat and the difficulty in your breathing. Once you are aware of this problem, make sure you don't control your breathing unconsciously. For those of you whose unconscious regulation of breathing is so serious that it leads to throat irritation, you can breathe through the mouth for a while before switching back to breathing through the nose. Continue to monitor the problem and make sure it does not recur. People who experience this condition usually regulate their breathing in the same manner when they silently chant Buddha's name during the day, so watch out for it during your practice. Step 4 is completed when the mind has stopped clinging to any sensory objects. Practitioners who are not troubled by breathing control can go directly to the next stage.

STEP 5: Achieving Single-Minded Concentration in Prostration to Buddha with Signless Mindfulness with Closed Eyes

Now you can carry out prostration to Buddha with signless mindfulness with one-pointed focus and closed eyes. The pure thought of Buddha is clear and distinct and you no longer cling to any visual form, sound, smell, taste, touch, or mental object. Do not be complacent. Continue to be diligent in the prostration practice and during the rest of your time keep up the Buddha's name recitation practice to further enhance your proficiency. With persistent practice, the pure thought of Buddha will continue without interruption and will be clearly present without the need to consciously restrain the mind to maintain single-pointed focus. You feel relaxed and refreshed when you prostrate rather than tense and restless. Practitioners who have practiced breath-counting meditation for years will find that the "abiding in one continuous pure thought" during prostration to Buddha with signless mindfulness is no different from "counting until there is nothing to count; leaving only a continuous thought"—a state of mental absorption achieved through breath-counting.

By now you will have absolute confidence in this Dharma-door and you can experience the mental state of being free from discursive thoughts while prostrating to Buddha with signless mindfulness. This is what I meant when I said in previous chapter that for those who have entered this state, it is the continuous abiding in one-pointed focus. Despite being able to reach this stage, you should keep up the mental recitation of Buddha's name alongside all daily activities. Do not be concerned if your recitation has slowed down significantly, as this reflects a state of mental absorption and is a sign of enhanced power of meditative concentration. Even when sometimes you feel so relaxed that you want to drop the mental recitation, do carry on the recitation while holding the thought of the Buddha in mind. As for practitioners who have practiced

Buddha-mindfulness through name recitation before, you do not need this recitation practice. You should constantly remind yourself to be mindful of the Buddha throughout the day without relying on any form, including the name of the Buddha.

STEP 6: Prostration to Buddha with Signless Mindfulness and Eyes Open

By now you should have built up your concentration and can overcome the grasping tendency of the eyes, you should start prostrating to Buddha with signless mindfulness of Buddha with your eyes open. Same as described above, prostrate to the Buddha for ten to twenty minutes every morning and evening. With your eyes open, maintain continuous mindfulness of the Buddha while prostrating. At first, you may still be occasionally distracted by visual objects. The image of the Buddha might appear in your mind's eye when you see the Buddha statue in front of you, or you may sometimes be compelled to take a glance at the objects on the offering table, a strand of hair, lint, or some patterns on the ground. When this happens, collect your mind and redirect your attention to whether the pure thought is broken or not. Move the focal point of your eyes away from all visual objects. In other words, while your eyes still see, they remain soft and the visual field is slightly blurry. Direct your mind inward and think about Buddha's Dharma-body dwelling in your mind. Focus all attention on prostrating and maintaining mindfulness, and all the while observe whether the pure thought is clear and distinct.

Practice diligently and consistently every day in this way to restrain your mental focus from scattering. In time you will be able to prostrate to the Buddha with single-pointed absorption, taking no notice of what comes into sight or within earshot. As the six sense objects (Note 11) no longer hinder and interfere with your prostration practice or mindfulness, the pace of your prostration will naturally quicken slightly as you are getting close to accomplishing this Dharma-door.

STEP 7: Signless Mindfulness of Buddha alongside all Daily Activities

When you are able to prostrate to Buddha with signless mindfulness undistracted by any sense objects (forms, sounds, ordors, tastes, tactile objects and mental phenomena) and in a tranquil, relaxed manner, replace the complementary mental recitation practice with signless mindfulness of Buddha alongside all daily activities; in other words, you are virtually practicing signless Buddha-mindfulness throughout the day. The Buddha you practice signless mindfulness with should be the same one you prostrate to during your morning and evening practice. Do not prostrate to Buddha Śākyamuni and hold Bodhisattva Avalokiteśvara in mind during the rest of the day, or else your meditative concentration will stop deepening or even regress. Nor should you be mindful of Buddha Śākyamuni some of the time and Buddha Amitābha the rest of the time, or be mindful of two or more Buddhas at the same time. You ought to concentrate on the Buddha or bodhisattva that you chose when you first began this practice and stick with him. Keeping of a clear, distinct, and pure thought of the Buddha (or the bodhisattva) you prostrate to continuously at all time in everyday life, without employing name, sounds, or images is what I call the signless mindfulness of Buddha, which is the elementary practice of Bodhisattva Mahāsthāmaprāpta's Dharma-door for perfect mastery through Buddha-mindfulness. It is certainly possible to reach this level of signless Buddha-mindfulness through name recitation as well, but only if you are equipped with sufficient and correct knowledge about samādhi training as well as a decent level of concentration. Except for a small number of people who have abundant wholesome roots, merits, and right conditions, rarely can one achieve this stage through name recitation.

You have almost accomplished signless Buddha-mindfulness at this point. Cherish your hard-earned skill. Do not allow your mind to go unbridled or revert back to the practice of name recitation. Just like those who practice name recitation, losing the thought of Buddha from time to time as you go about your everyday business is unavoidable. Nonetheless, if you have learned the Buddha Dharma for decades without any significant progress, upon reaching this stage you must have realized how blessed you are to have come upon this incredible method. Having experienced the amazing benefits of this Dharma-door, you will not regress from it but constantly remind yourself to bring up the mindfulness of Buddha during the day. It is normal to lose the mindfulness during conversations as you have to listen to others and come up with replies. Moreover, you may want to drop the mindfulness temporarily when you are thinking over personal or business matters. And if your vocation or job is potentially dangerous or hazardous, you should give full attention to your work rather than carrying out Buddha-mindfulness. Before falling asleep every night, you can practice signless Buddha-mindfulness in a relaxed manner while lying comfortably in bed and let yourself fall asleep with it. Please be advised that despite having reached this stage, you should continue your practice of signless Buddha-mindfulness prostration every morning and evening with one-pointed concentration. Your practice at this stage is accomplished when you can maintain signless mindfulness during most of your waking hours.

The accomplishment of this stage comes with strong Dharma-joy. If it takes more than two months to complete this stage, the Dharma-joy will be slightly weaker. Generally speaking, the longer it takes to reach this stage, the weaker the Dharma-joy felt; if it takes six months or longer, then there is hardly any Dharma-joy even though the skill level acquired is the same. Nonetheless, even if you have accomplished this Dharma-door swiftly, the intense Dharma-joy you feel will gradually fade away as you get used to it, so do not worry about it when that happens.

STEP 8: Prostrate to Multiple Buddhas and Bodhisattvas

In the beginning of this stage, continue to prostrate to the one Buddha or bodhisattva of your choice every morning. Again, the prostration should be accompanied by a yearning for Buddha without name or image. Throughout the rest of the day, be mindful of the same Buddha or bodhisattva alongside all daily activities. In the evening prostration session, prostrate to multiple Buddhas or bodhisattvas. Before you start, pick three to six Buddhas or bodhisattvas and arrange them in a fixed order. As a rule of thumb, Buddhas should come before bodhisattvas. Also, the first one on your list must be Buddha Śākyamuni, for all Buddhist learners in this world are His disciples and are able to cultivate the Dharma because of him. Therefore, to show gratitude to the source of our wisdom, we should prostrate first to the World-Honored One, Buddha Śākyamuni. You are free to choose another two to five Buddhas or bodhisattvas after Buddha Śākyamuni.

Once the order of prostration is set it should not be altered any more. Then you start to prostrate to these Buddhas and bodhisattvas in your evening session in tandem with signless mindfulness. Make three prostrations to each Buddha or bodhisattva within ten to twenty minutes. If time has run out before you finish prostrating to all Buddhas and bodhisattvas, slowly complete all prostrations according to the set order. When choosing Buddhas or bodhisattvas to whom you feel an affinity with, choose no fewer than three and at most six. The efficacy of this training is limited if you prostrate to fewer than three Buddhas or bodhisattvas. On the other hand, if you prostrate to more than six, the training is counterproductive, since your mind would have to pay too

111

much attention on the order of prostration and become easily distracted as a result.

The purpose of this expedient method is to train your mind to be more sensitive and discerning, such that you can not only acquire the ability to distinguish a wordless thought (*huatou*) but also the ability to carry out "meditative contemplation" (Note 12) during Chan contemplation.

In your evening session of prostrations, you should, as always, hold in mind a pure thought of the Buddhas and bodhisattvas without using names, images, or sounds, yet still being able to clearly differentiate during each prostration which is the thought of Buddha Śākyamuni, which is the thought of Buddha Amitābha, Bodhisattva Avalokiteśvara, or Bodhisattva Mahāsthāmaprāpta. In addition, you should be able to clearly identify the differences between the characteristic of the former thought and the subsequent one.

When you first enter this stage, you should prostrate to the one Buddha or bodhisattva you have chosen in the morning and only prostrate to multiple Buddhas and bodhisattvas in the evening. This is because when you first accomplished Step 7, your mind's power of meditative concentration is not stable and firm yet. Because of this, when you first made the transition to this stage, you still need to rely on the prostration practice every morning to strengthen the complementary signless Buddha-mindfulness practice that you perform during the rest of the day. If you start prostrating to multiple Buddhas in both morning and evening right away, your level of concentration may stop deepening. Hence, it is recommended that you first continue to prostrate to one Buddha in the morning to enhance your level of in-motion concentration through single-minded mindfulness. This will ensure swift achievement of unbroken signless Buddha-mindfulness in daily life.

Practice in this way for two to four weeks until you have reached the point that the more active you are physically, the clearer your signless mindfulness of Buddha is. Then you can proceed to prostrating to multiple Buddhas and bodhisattvas in both mornings and evenings. The order must be the same in both the morning and evening practice, and the Buddha or bodhisattva you practice signless mindfulness with in daily life must also remain the same. Making frequent changes to your choices is highly detrimental to your practice.

When you prostrate to multiple Buddhas, prostrate to each of them three times, no more and no less. More than three times, the differences between the thoughts cannot be clearly distinguished. Less than three times, your mind would become easily distracted and your concentration cannot deepen. At first you tend to forget how many times you have already prostrated. You may mistake the first prostration for the second one, or the third prostration for the second one. When you are confused or unsure about the number of prostrations you have made, just take what you believe to be right at that moment. There is no need to feel bad about forgetting the number of prostration. Self-reproach will only undermine your practice.

Besides, the "number of prostrations" is a concept predicated on the existence of a physical body and its action. Yet, your body and its action are merely instruments to train your mind. As long as you can train your mind to concentrate on one pure thought and can make subtle distinction, it does not matter whether you are correct about how many times you have prostrated. What is important is whether you are able to make clear distinction between thoughts. If you lost count of the number of times you have prostrated, all you have to do is to promptly decide on a number you believe to be right at the moment and continue your prostration. Do not allow the feeling of self-criticism to affect the on-going practice.

When you are mentally keeping track of the number of prostrations, neither the image nor the sound of the numbers "one, two, three" should appear in your mind. Furthermore, you should have a clear awareness of both how many times you have prostrated as well as which Buddha you are prostrating to. After prostrating three times to one Buddha or bodhisattva, there should not be the thought of "I am going to prostrate to Bodhisattva Mahāsthāmaprāpta next." Without the name of the Buddha or the number of prostrations arising in your mind, you should switch directly to the pure thought of the next Buddha or bodhisattva and know that this is the first prostration. In other words, the thought of the Buddha or bodhisattva exists clearly and distinctively together with the "knowing" that "this is the first prostration." With persistent practice, you will be able to distinguish clearly which Buddha or bodhisattva you are prostrating to right now and how many times you have prostrated to him already. Also, as your proficiency improves, you will be able to differentiate clearly the thought of the previous Buddha from the thought of the next Buddha.

STEP 9: Seek not Afar for the "Buddha"

Upon completion of Step 8, you know very well that you are about to achieve the Dharma-door of signless Buddha-mindfulness. Despite this exhilarating prospect, do not allow self-content or, even worse, self-conceit to overpower you. Swell with self-contentment and you will stop your prostration practice, and as a result, the level of your meditative concentration will stagnate. It is critical to understand that your power of in-motion concentration can only deepen through continuous practice of signless Buddha-mindfulness in tandem with prostration practice. When, out of self-content, you allow your practice to slack off, your power of meditative concentration will surely decline, unless you are of a sharp capacity, have already cultivated samādhi for eons, or if your power of meditative concentration has already surpassed this level. Therefore, continue your prostrations every morning and evening conscientiously.

Self-conceit, on the other hand, breeds a "mind of discrimination," by which I mean you will hold yourself above others and think that they should all follow your example. Harboring this discriminatory mentality, you will treat others with a prideful mind and miss out on the benefits of Dharma cultivation. Hence, upon reaching this stage, it is very important to eliminate self-content, self-conceit and the prideful mind. Continue your practice in earnest as before to enhance your proficiency, and your mind will become more lucid and tranquil. Eventually, signless mindfulness of Buddha will abide in your mind clearly, distinctly, and effortlessly during your morning and evening prostration practice. As well, you can also make clear distinction between the thoughts of prostrating to one Buddha and the next. During prostrations, you are relaxed and tranquil, and never lose count of the number of times you have prostrated. Numbers do not arise in your mind in the form of images or sounds anymore. In addition, you are able to maintain signless mindfulness with great ease at any time and in any circumstance during your hectic life. You can remain in signless Buddha-mindfulness spontaneously and effortlessly even when you are talking, handling personal or business matters, or thinking over something.

At this stage, your mind is focused and lucid, and you have the conviction that the "Buddha" is within this mind and body. As the saying goes: "Do not seek for the Buddha afar at Vulture Peak, Vulture Peak is none other than my mind." You realize that this thought of signless mindfulness of Buddha is actually an inward seeking. If you have been yearning for Buddha Śākyamuni, you feel that he is actually in your own mind, not even a hair's breadth away. This is a realization that you will come to no matter which Buddha or bodhisattva you are mindful of.

By now, when you walk in the streets, whether you are looking at a dog or a person, they are both Buddha to you. Whatever comes into sight is none other than the thought of Buddha even though there is no name, no sound, nor image of Buddha. Likewise, whatever you hear throughout the day is the calling to the Buddha, even though the sound of Buddha's name does not appear in your mind. The *Amitābha Sūtra* contains the following description of the Pure Land of Ultimate Bliss: "...when the soft wind blows, the rows of jeweled trees and jeweled nets give forth subtle and wonderful sounds....All those who hear these sounds naturally bring forth in their hearts mindfulness of the Buddha, mindfulness of the Dharma, and mindfulness of the Sangha." What you experience now is no different from the above description. Even though there are no rows of jeweled trees or jeweled nets that produce subtle and wonderful sounds in this world of five turbidities known as "patient endurance," by cultivating the Dharma-door for perfect mastery through Buddha-mindfulness, you are able to spontaneously bring forth the mindfulness of Buddha upon hearing any noise. There are no thoughts that are not the mindfulness of Buddha.

The Dharma-joy one experiences at this stage of practice is the most intense. A practitioner who has reached this stage within six weeks of practice through utmost effort experiences Dharma-joy that is so intense that he feels rapturous. He will enthusiastically encourage anyone he comes upon to practice this Dharma-door, and out of compassion, wishes that everyone can enter the Mind-Only

Pure Land or can be reborn in the pure lands of Buddhas through this Dharma-door. Unlike ordinary Buddhist learners who often feel unsure of or are stuck in their cultivation, he knows with absolute certainty that he can take rebirth in the Pure Land of Ultimate Bliss. On the other hand, if you were originally a Chan practitioner, upon reaching this stage you will have acquired the ability to contemplate a *huatou* and perform meditative contemplation. In other words, the "gateless gate" is right in front of you. Overjoyed with this accomplishment, you will wish for all Buddhist disciples to reach the gateless gate through signless Buddha-mindfulness as well.

Since it usually takes about three full months for an average practitioner to reach Step 9, the Dharma-joy experienced is usually less intense. Without due diligence, it could take four or five months, or even years before one accomplishes this Dharma-door. But even a practitioner of duller capacity is able to reach this stage within six months through industrious practice, but the Dharma-joy felt will be rather weak.

Please be advised that you must not skip the necessary steps and stages in your practice to hasten your progress. Nor should you become attached to the Dharma-joy. Or else you will find to your dismay that being impatient to experience and having attachment to Dharma-joy only serve to delay rather than quicken your progress. In any case, the Dharma-joy you experience is merely a perceived emotion. Like the ecstatic joy one feels when one wins the lottery, the initial exhilaration will inevitably and gradually fade away as it is by nature a transient rather than eternal kind of bliss. Your cultivation should not be motivated by the desire for Dharma-joy. Rather, set the attainment of ultimate liberation as your aim and goal, as it is a purpose that is conducive to your practice.

STEP 10: Cultivate Meditative Concentration both in Motion and in Stillness

Though you have mastered signless mindfulness of Buddha now, please do not be satisfied with your achievement. Upon careful introspection, you will notice that the pure thought of Buddha is fuzzier when you are thinking or talking. This can be remedied by allocating equal attention to internal absorption and external discernment (Note 13) during conversation and contemplation. The better you can allocate equal attention to both, the clearer is the pure thought of the Buddha. To accomplish this, in addition to the twice a day prostrations as well as maintaining signless Buddha-mindfulness throughout the day, you need also to participate in group practices, where you observe the mindfulness while chanting the Buddha's name aloud, until the mindfulness is unaffected by the oral recitation but become unified with it in a state of clarity (this can be practiced at home as well). On top of that, practice sitting meditate for an hour every day, during which you settle your mind in Buddha-mindfulness without letting it grow dull and observe how it changes from coarse to fine. These two practices are designed to strengthen your power of meditative concentration in stillness based upon the power of in-motion concentration you already possess. All Buddhist learners who wish to "enter the path" swiftly must take up these two different modes of samādhi training.

If you seek to attain Buddha-Mindfulness Samādhi and realize the Mind-Only Pure Land, you must also complement your everyday in-motion practice of signless mindfulness with a daily session of signless Buddha-mindfulness in sitting meditation. This is because the specific characteristics of samādhi has to be cultivated through sitting meditation. During the meditation practice, if you can perform signless Buddha-mindfulness while keeping your body steady and firm, rein in all six sensory faculties and abiding in one continuous pure thought, and if you can maintain this practice as a daily routine, you will enter samādhi once your dispositional hindrances have been eliminated. Those who further their practice diligently will become proficient in the samādhi and gradually attain the myriad meritorious qualities that come with Buddha-mindfulness. They will enter deep into the profound and wondrous states in Bodhisattva Mahāsthāmaprāpta's Dharma-door for perfect mastery through Buddha-mindfulness and gradually attain the Great Śūraṅgama Samādhi. Please refer to the *Śūraṅgama Sūtra* for details if you are interested in learning about the various states of the Great Śūraṅgama Samādhi as well as the states associated with the realization of self-nature.

Upon the completion of Step 10, you can clearly observe the pure thought of signless mindfulness of Buddha in your mind at any time, regardless whether you are in stillness or in motion. Like the herding of cows, when the cows have been completely domesticated they will follow the order of the herder. You will therefore suddenly realize "the first sudden instance of awareness [of an object]" described in the scriptures. While this marks the perfect mastery of signless Buddha-mindfulness, what you have accomplished is merely the elementary practice of Bodhisattva Mahāsthāmaprāpta's Dharma-door for perfect mastery through Buddha-mindfulness.

Having mastered signless Buddha-mindfulness, if you want to be reborn in any pure lands of Buddhas, once daily all you need to do is to chant the Buddha's name in front of his image or statue, or to the sky above, while calling to mind the Four Vast Vows as well as the specific vows of the particular Buddha whose pure land you want to be reborn in. For instance, if you seek rebirth in Buddha Amitābha's Pure Land of Ultimate Bliss, then among the forty-eight specific vows of Buddha Amitābha, you should be mindful of the ones that correspond to your own. If you wish to be reborn in Buddha Bhaiṣajyaguru's Pure Land of Lapis Lazuli Light in the East, be mindful of the vows among His twelve specific vows that correspond with your own. On top of that, dedicate the virtues of your daily practice to the rebirth in that Buddha land at the end of life. During all other times, focus on yearning for the Buddha whose pure land you seek to take rebirth in. Upon the end of your lifetime, you will receive advance notice from him, and seven days later, he will appear in front of you, take your hand, and make sure you go to the pure land peacefully without apprehension.

This is indeed the dream of all Pure Land practitioners who practice Buddha-mindfulness.

If, having secured rebirth in Buddha's pure land by achieving one-pointed focus without distractive thoughts, you would like to further your cultivation of the Buddha Dharma in this life, then you should extend the hours of meditation and go deeper into the Dharma-door for perfect mastery through Buddha-mindfulness. Depending on the depth of your good roots and diligence, you may gradually attain the various states of liberation in the Great Śūraṅgama Samādhi and the numerous kinds of Buddha-mindfulness Samādhi, the wonders of which are beyond my ability to describe and illustrate.

As mentioned earlier, the Dharma-door for perfect mastery through Buddha-mindfulness taught by Bodhisattva Mahāsthāmaprāpta can be practiced at all levels from easy to profound. In other words, bodhisattvas at any one of the fifty-two stages of the bodhisattva path, from the ten Faith stages all the way to those at the stages of Virtual Enlightenment and Sublime Enlightenment, can practice this Dharma-door; this one Dharma-door can produce different levels of attainment depending on the individual. For instance, according to the Śūraṅgama Sūtra, a bodhisattva who has extinguished the perception-aggregate and has started to extinguish or have already extinguished the domain of the formation-aggregate will have surpassed the attainment of an arhat. If he further enters the domain of the consciousness-aggregate and extinguishes it, he will have completed the Tenth Ground and become a Virtual-Enlightenment bodhisattva. Between the most elementary level of signless Buddha-mindfulness and the extinguishment of the consciousness-aggregate, the most profound level, there are myriads of attainments and states to be realized. Therefore, we should set our minds on assiduously cultivating all of the various levels of the liberation states illustrated in the sūtra with the spirit of "the loftier the goal, the stronger the determination to achieve it." Please do not be satisfied with your meager attainment and proclaim that you have achieved Bodhisattva Mahāsthāmaprāpta's Dharma-door for perfect mastery through Buddha-mindfulness; for this deed amounts to false speech. As always, continue your practice humbly and make offerings and prostrations earnestly and sincerely to Buddha Śākyamuni as well as the Buddha or bodhisattva with whom you practice mindfulness.

Afterword

1. The mastery of signless Buddha-mindfulness imparts a sense of self-assurance in a practitioner. He will be confident that he is on the right track of Dharma cultivation. He will no longer be plagued by skeptical doubts and misgivings and therefore can naturally forge ahead with his practice.

2. Those who originally practiced Chan and subsequently switched to this method will acquire the ability to guard a *huatou* upon the successful completion of Step 7. At this time, the practitioner may try out this newfound ability but should limit the attempt to only once or twice. The practitioner should continue to enhance his power of meditative concentration through signless Buddha-mindfulness and the prostration practice; do not switch back to Chan contemplation until one has completed Step 9 and 10. The reason is that it is much easier to rein in all six sense faculties and abide in a pure thought of Buddha during these signless practices since one will be blessed with Buddha's and bodhisattvas' support and reinforced by one's own faith in them. Chan contemplation and the guarding of *huatou*, on the contrary, rely much less on blessings but more on one's own skill set and confidence (in fact blessings from Buddhas and bodhisattvas are still present but the practitioner's effort plays a more important role in the process; the practitioner will understand this fact when

he realizes his self-nature). Thus, in addition to a higher level of meditative concentration and a more sensitive and discerning mind, a Chan practitioner must also have stronger confidence in his own ability to achieve awakening. Upon accomplishing Step 9 and 10, a Chan practitioner's power of meditative concentration and confidence will be sufficient and it will therefore be easy for him to generate the sense of Chan doubt and enter into the "mass of doubt" if he switches to Chan contemplation at these junctures. Meanwhile, the Chan practitioner should obtain right views regarding Chan contemplation by perusing literature of the Chan school written by virtuous and wise teachers. They should also acquaint themselves and study with enlightened mentors. This will prevent one from going down the wrong path and avoid incurring wasted time and efforts.

For practitioners who have been contemplating a *huatou* (or a *huawei*), please refer to the instructions of Venerable Xuyun for the definition of *huatou* and the correct way to practice. Alternatively, one may refer to the explanation given in the Introduction (chapter 1). Practitioners should be delighted to be able to gain the ability from these sources and move on to the excruciating and mind-racking phase of Chan contemplation, since the moment of awakening could just be around the corner.

3. A practitioner who has always practiced the Pure Land methods should be able to maintain mental absorption both in motion and in stillness as a result of following through this Dharma-door of signless Buddha-

mindfulness. When his conditions mature, a sense of doubt will spontaneously spring up either in motion or in stillness, ushering him into the stage of contemplative Buddha-mindfulness. In each and every thought, the practitioner will seek to answer the question "Who is bearing the Buddha in mind?" There is no need to be alarmed when this happens and one should not resist this sense of doubt. This is the critical moment and the initial sign of "spontaneous awakening to the True Mind without employing skillful means" described in "Bodhisattva Mahāsthāmaprāpta's Dharma-door for Perfect Mastery through Buddha-Mindfulness." This mental query is precisely what the sense of doubt in Chan contemplation. Once this doubt has arisen, the practitioner should probe deeper into the *huatou* of "Who is bearing the Buddha in mind?" When conditions mature, the practitioner will, in one corresponding thought, realize his origin before being born, which may seem surprisingly plain and ordinary. This awakening can also happen when one is in a state of stillness or even perhaps upon bumping into or simply knocking over something. This is how one "spontaneously awakens to the True Mind without employing skillful means," a goal for which tens and thousands of Chan practitioners strive without success. In this practice, since the practitioner has first acquired solid, non-regressing power of in-motion concentration, he will not backslide from this awakening once he has achieved it. This enables the practitioner to eliminate the three fetters, reduce greed, aversion and delusion, and join the ranks of non-retrogressing bodhisattvas.

Henceforth the practitioner can naturally develop correct views based upon his realization and decipher most of the confusing *gong'ans* presented by Chan patriarchs. As well, the practitioner will attain many benefits and meritorious qualities from the experiences of daily life, from cultivation of the Buddha Dharma, reading sūtras and scriptures, as well as from the state of liberation. This is how the dual cultivation of Chan and Pure Land can enable a practitioner to enter the "principle" by means of mindfulness of Buddha. This achievement comes with countless benefits; a discussion is not included here since they are beyond the scope of this book. I have only mentioned a few to inspire and motivate fellow practitioners. Having reached this stage, one would understand the following words of Chan Master Daoxin:

> With continuous yearning for Buddha, the mind's tenacious clinging no longer arises, all appearances cease, all phenomena are equal and non-dual. Upon entering this stage, the mind of Buddha-mindfulness shall wilt but it is unnecessary to revive it. Guard this mind of non-duality, which is the Tathāgata's true body of dharma-nature, also referred to as the True Dharma, Buddha-nature, true essence and limit of reality of all phenomena, pure land, bodhi, diamond samādhi, fundamental awareness, and so forth.
>
> 常憶念佛，攀緣不起，則眠然無相、平等不二。入此位中，憶佛心謝、更不須徵，即看此等心，既是如來真實法性之身，亦名正法，

亦名佛性，亦名諸法實性實際，亦名淨土，
亦名菩提、金剛三昧、本覺等。[*Record of the
Masters and Disciples of the Laṅkāvatāra Sūtra*
楞伽師資記. CBETA, T85, no. 2837, 1287a16-19]

4. Whether the practitioner has awakened to "the principle" through Chan contemplation or Buddha-mindfulness, having seen the Buddha-nature, he should consult with someone who has truly seen the path. This is to avoid the mistaking of a delusive awakening or a samādhi state for the state of true awakening. Please pay attention to these fine points, or else it might be too late to rectify the fault if impermanence sneaks up on you.

5. I am a rather undistinguished individual and am unassociated with the people and affairs in the Buddhist community. I am using the name Xiao Pingshi (蕭平實) to propagate this Dharma-door that most people find hard to believe and practice, so as to elucidate the correct way to enter the Dharma-door for perfect mastery through Buddha-mindfulness. Although I have devised many expedients to facilitate its practice, I'm afraid that not many people will have faith in it, and even fewer will practice in accordance to the instructions I set forth. Practitioners who accept and follow the steps of cultivation in this book must have cultivated the Buddha Dharma for many lifetimes and accumulated a mature level of faith and abundant wholesome roots. They will surely and quickly master the signless mindfulness of Buddha.

6. I have some but meager attainment in Chan contemplation. Since I still need to focus on furthering my own practice, I will not be able to deliver lectures, seminars, and talks in different places. Practitioners who wish to but are unable to comprehend this Dharma-door of signless Buddha-mindfulness after reading this book should repent their past transgressions in front of Buddha, diligently cultivate the three blessed pure deeds, and constantly ponder over the contents of this book. Additionally, they should support Buddhist institutions in the circulation of this book and make this sincere vow in front of the Buddha: "I am willing to cultivate the bodhisattva path and save sentient beings in each and every lifetime. If I can accomplish this Dharma-door, I will propagate it and help others to accomplish it and share its benefits." After taking this vow, they should beseech Buddha Śākyamuni, Bodhisattva Avalokiteśvara, Bodhisattva Mahāsthāmaprāpta for their compassionate blessings. Practitioners should also mull over the contents of this book over and again while carrying out prostration to Buddha with signless mindfulness every day to experience it in depth. As karmic hindrances gradually diminish, one will come to understand this method and derive tremendous benefits from it.

I have gone over the underlying principles and the expedient means of signless Buddha-mindfulness in tedious repetitions, and explained all that I know about this Dharma-door—its essence and cultivation—in exhaustive detail, almost to the point of a nagging parent. It is my greatest hope that practitioners can understand and take up this Dharma-door in actual practice, but with the exception of those who I will be acquainted with in a practice group situation, I shall not make myself available for any inquiries regarding this book. I shall focus myself on furthering my Dharma cultivation such that I can benefit more people in the future. I appreciate your understanding of my decision and apologize to all readers and practitioners for not being able to personally answer any questions.

7. I will humbly accept all written critiques and comments on this book but will not respond to any. There are two reasons for this decision: Firstly, I need to make myself available for students in my practice group. Secondly, I am still far from the cultivation objective I aim to reach in this life. My years are limited whilst impermanence catches up swiftly, so I'd rather not spend my time making replies and explanations. I beg all virtuous and wise teachers to excuse my situation and I'm deeply appreciative of your understanding.

8. In regard to the numerous Chan practitioners out there, I apologize that I cannot extensively expound my shallow experience in Chan contemplation given my limited capacity. I offer the following verse as an apology:

> *Frantically searching for a master throughout remote lands,*
> *As if carrying the weight of one's dying parents on hunched back,*
> *Reaching Vulture Peak, there is nothing else to be found,*
> *Naught but the scent of lotuses in the pond just*

beyond the front door.

9. The publication of this book would have been impossible without the help from Xu Guochuan (許 果 川), Liu Jinshan (劉 近 山), Zhang Guoyuan (張 果 圜), Liang Chuanfu (梁傳輔), as well as many others, who, despite their busy schedules, assisted in the polishing, proofreading, copying, editing of the draft, typesetting, etc. Their hard work and enthusiastic dedication to the welfare of sentient beings deserve heartfelt and boundless appreciation.

Xiao Pingshi
Feb 28, 1992

Extended Afterword

The publication of this book has been delayed by certain conditions until now. But during this delay, three fellow practitioners achieved awakening just before December 1st, 1992, and personally verified that this Dharma-door can definitely enable one to realize one's Buddha-nature by "spontaneous awakening to the True Mind without employing skillful means." The course of their cultivation and the benefits they obtained were in full accordance with the elaborations in this book. Before the aforementioned three practitioners, another practitioner who contemplated Chan after mastering signless Buddha-mindfulness also broke through Chan contemplation and experienced all the benefits that came with it. To this day, these four people have not regressed from the state of awakening and can see their intrinsic Buddha-nature anytime and anywhere.

From the time I began lecturing on the practice of signless mindfulness of Buddha until these four practitioners' seeing their intrinsic Buddha-nature, only fifteen months had lapsed. In time, more practitioners will follow their steps. Risking the label of self-promoting, I deliberately draw attention to their emboldening achievements which further attest the veracity of Bodhisattva Mahāsthāmaprāpta's words that this method enables "spontaneous awakening to the True Mind without any other skillful means than the recollection and mindfulness of Buddha."

Moreover, among the three practitioners who

achieved awakening through Buddha-mindfulness, the last one was a woman with only elementary education who had never heard of or read about Chan contemplation before. She can now properly explain the Dharma to people and her reasoning never deviates from the Middle Way. The transformation cannot be more astonishing, considering her previous timidity and ineptness in Dharma enquiry. This example is meant to inspire and motivate the small number of Buddha-mindfulness practitioners who have little education and have serious lack of confidence to practice this Dharma-door assiduously and conscientiously. I want to congratulate in advance all who are to follow the footsteps of those four practitioners and I eagerly look forward to your accomplishments.

Supplemented by,
Xiao Pingshi
February 2, 1993

Further Remarks

A few more words I must share. Before this book went to print, around the time of the second proofreading and after typesetting, another three practitioners awakened to the True Mind through *huatou* contemplation and another practitioner was able to uncover his True Mind and achieve awakening through no other aids apart from the practice of signless Buddha-mindfulness. All of them realized the Buddha-nature and "returned to the origin of existence." It is said in the sūtras that, "Those have seen the path may be female but are also regarded as worthy men." Hence, although all three of the aforementioned practitioners were women, I address them as Dharma brothers all the same.

The realization of the True Mind and seeing of the Buddha-nature have become a disfavored subject for contemporary Buddhists. In spite of this strong aversion, I raise this topic here for the purpose of instilling great faith in all Buddhist learners. Living in the time of and within the social milieu of the Dharma-ending age does not necessarily mean that we are of an inferior capacity or limited aspirations. Everybody's intrinsic Buddha-nature is unstirred and self-existing, and has always been so. If one can continuously abide in the one pure thought while in motion, awakening will come in one sudden and immediately self-evident thought. Wisdom will emerge spontaneously and he will summarily become one who knows his "original self." Given such an awakening, there is no distinction of Dharma-ending or not! If these claims I made shall incur slanderous remarks against me, I will gladly accept them. I am satisfied as long as my words can build up great faith in some of the Buddhist learners out there. This is my purpose in putting together these additional remarks.

Holder of the Bodhisattva Precepts
Xiao Pingshi
Feb 20, 1993

Notes

Note 1.: According to the *Sūtra on the Contemplation of Buddha Amitāyus*, the three grades of the lowest level of rebirth in the Pure Land of Ultimate Bliss are reserved for beings who have committed all kinds of unwholesome deeds but did not slander the Mahāyāna Dharma. Aided by the expedient powers of Buddha Amitābha, they will become Mahāyāna bodhisattvas and attain fruitions below the First Ground after their rebirth in the Pure Land. The realm they live in is one where ordinary people and saints mingle; it is called the Realm Inhabited by Both Ordinary and Saints. This kind of rebirth is of a lower rank.

The three grades of the middle level are to receive and embrace sentient beings with the disposition of a hearer (*śrāvaka*) through the expedient powers of Buddha Amitābha. These sentient beings will attain various fruitions of the hearer's vehicle (*śrāvakayāna*) and realize the nirvana with remainder in the Pure Land. Insofar that their abode in the Pure Land is an expedient manifestation of Buddha Amitābha, it is referred to as the Realm of Expedients and Remainder. This kind of rebirth is of the middle rank.

The three grades of the highest level of rebirth exclusively receive and embrace sentient beings with the capacity and disposition of Mahāyāna bodhisattvas—from those who have already seen the Buddha-nature to those who have merely brought forth the resolution to achieve the unsurpassed Buddhahood-Way. These sentient beings have realized the ultimate truth (i.e. realized the emptiness, the self-nature and the dharma-nature); or have simply comprehended the ultimate truth without fear; or have brought forth the resolve to attain Buddhahood. They will attain fruitions above the First Ground and will partially realize the Dharma-body. Their abode in the Pure Land is called the Realm of True Reward and Adornment. This kind of rebirth is of the highest rank.

It should not be interpreted that each of these three realms in the Pure Land—the Realm Inhabited by Both the Ordinary and the Saints, the Realm of Expedients and Remainder, the Realm of True Reward and Adornment— consists of nine grades of rebirth.

Note 2. Acquiescence to non-arising (*anutpannakṣāntika*; 無生忍): the attaining of partial or ultimate realization of liberation are both considered acquiescence to non-arising.

Note 3. Adept (*aśaikṣa*; 無學): A person who has yet to perfect his cultivation and still has fruitions to attain is called a learner (學人). Practitioners who have attained ultimate liberation and have personally realized the Path to Liberation with perfect understanding are referred to as an adept.

Note 4. Buddha-Mindfulness Samādhi (念佛三昧): There are numerous kinds of Buddha-Mindfulness Samādhi. For details please refer to the section "Buddha-Mindfulness Samādhi (念 佛 三 昧 品)" in Volume 43 of the *Mahāvaipulyamahāsaṃnipāta Sūtra* (大方等大集經; T13, no. 397), the *Bodhisattva-buddhānusmṛti-samādhi Sūtra* (菩薩念佛三昧經; T13, no. 414), or the *Mahāvaipulya-*

mahāsaṃnipāta-bodhisattva-buddhānusmṛti-samādhi (大方等大集菩薩念佛三昧分; T13, no. 415), all of which are found in the Mahāsaṃnipāta Division of the Taisho Tripiṭaka.Buddha-Mindfulness Samādhis usually refer to the mindfulness of the three bodies of Buddha: the emanation-body, the reward-body, and the Dharma-body. Signless mindfulness of Buddha is one way to attain Buddha-Mindfulness Samādhi; particularly, it is one of the numerous ways to attain Buddha-Mindfulness Samādhis through the mindfulness of Buddha's Dharma-body. The state of samādhi one enters by means of the mindfulness of Buddha is also called the Buddha-Mindfulness Samādhi.

Note 5. Most practitioners who practice Buddha-mindfulness through the recitation of Buddha's name would be intimidated by the notion of samādhi training. They do not know that recitation of Buddha's name actually is one of the many methods to cultivate samādhi. In Vol. 4 of the *Commentaries on the Sūtra on the Contemplation of Buddha Amitāyus*, we can find the following statements:

> ...to single-mindedly recite the name of Buddha Amitābha while walking, resting, sitting, or lying down, and abide in this in every thought regardless of the length of time, is the deed of right concentration.

> 一心專念彌陀名號，行住坐臥、不問時節久近、念念不舍者，是名正定之業。[*Guan wuliangfo jing shu* 觀無量壽佛經疏: CBETA, T37, no. 1753, vol. 4, 272a28]

Buddhist patriarchs throughout history have explained

extensively the critical importance of samādhi cultivation. The following words by Master Huiyuan (廬山慧遠; 334–416), the founding patriarch of the Pure Land, found in the preface of the *Huiyuan Fashi Wenchao Paiyin Liutong* (慧遠法師文鈔排印流通), proves the significance of samādhi training for Pure Land practitioners:

...up to the twenty-eighth day of the seventh lunar month in the fifteenth year (year of Gengyin) of the Taiyuan reign period, [Huiyuan] formed a group with one hundred and twenty-three practitioners, comprised of both monastics and lay Buddhists, who seek rebirth in the Western Pure Land of Ultimate Bliss by practicing Buddha-mindfulness. All participants experienced auspicious signs near the end of their lives and all achieved rebirth in the Pure Land. The success of these participants ... was owed to the teachings of Venerable Huiyuan as well as their own diligent effort and support for one another. These one hundred and twenty-three people were only the earliest participants of the practice group. Throughout the remaining thirty or more years of the Master's life, the number of people who were able to practice the pure Dharma, attain samādhi and take rebirth in the Pure Land with his help were uncountable.

至太元十五年庚寅七月二十八日，（慧遠）與緇素一百二十三人結社念佛，求生西方。此諸人等、於臨終時皆有瑞應，皆得往生。良由諸人…. 蒙遠公開導、及諸友切磋琢磨之力，故獲此益。此系最初結社之人，若終公之世三十余年之內，蒙其法化而修淨業、得三昧而登蓮邦者，何可勝數。

[Master Yin Guang 印光法師, "Jin Lianzong Chuzu Lushan Huiyuan Fashi Wenchan 晉蓮宗初祖廬山慧遠法師文鈔." In *Yinguan Fashi Wenchao Xubian* 印光法師文抄續編, p.482. Taipei: Hwa Dzan Pure Land Teachings Propagation Foundation, 2010.]

In addition, the Appendix of *Huiyuan Fashi Wenchao* (慧遠法師文鈔) says:

...the Master had lived in the mountains for three decades, during which he never set foot in the mundane world but occupied himself with diligent practice of the Pure Land. In the first eleven years, he **cleared his mind and tied his thoughts to the Buddha** and thrice saw the sacred appearance [of Buddha Amitābha]. Being a modest and prudent person, he did not mention anything to other people. In one of the seventh lunar month during the subsequent nineteen years, he was at the eastern shrine alcove of the Prajñā Terrace one evening, and **upon exiting samādhi**, he saw Buddha Amitābha's body filling up the void flanked by Bodhisattvas Avalokiteśvara and Mahāsthāmaprāpta. There were also embodiment Buddhas in the halo surrounding Buddha Amitābha. Master also saw fourteen streams of radiant water flowing from top to bottom, all of which were preaching the truth of sufferings, emptiness, impermanence and non-self. The Buddha said to him: "I have come to console you with the power of my original vows. You will be born into my land in seven days..."

...師居山三十年，跡不入俗，唯以淨土克勤於念。

141

初十一年，澄心系想，三睹聖相，沈濃不言。後
十九年七月晦夕，於般若台之東龕，方從定起，
見阿彌陀佛身滿虛空，圓光之中有諸化佛，觀音
勢至左右侍立。又見水流光明分十四支，流注上
下，演說苦空無常無我之音。佛告之曰：我以本
願力故，來安慰汝，汝後七日當生我國⋯。
[CBETA, X78, no. 1543, 113b14]

According to these accounts, the one hundred and twenty-three participants of the practice group founded by the first patriarch of Pure Land were able to achieve rebirth in the Pure Land of Ultimate Bliss because they received Master Huiyuan's teachings and improved their practice through diligent practice and support from one another. As for Master Huiyuan himself, he practiced Buddha-mindfulness primarily by "**focusing on contemplation and quieting thoughts,**" whereby he saw the Buddha three times and received advance notice of his rebirth in the Pure Land seven days before his passing. He had a vision of the Buddha after **coming out of a state of one-pointed absorption of Buddha-mindfulness**.

These accounts of Master Huiyuan demonstrate that while it is possible to attain rebirth in the Pure Land of Ultimate Bliss through recitation of Buddha's name, the primary application of this practice is to rid the mind of discursive thoughts as well as its tenacious habit of clinging. The author believes that Pure Land practitioners can employ recitation of Buddha's name as an entrance expedient. Yet after spending some time on this method, they should move on to the "focusing on contemplation and quieting thoughts" method adopted by Venerable Huiyuan. Signless Buddha-mindfulness is an excellent expedient to ensure swift mastery of "focusing on contemplation and quieting thoughts." Accomplishment of this Dharma-door used by Master Huiyuan secures not only rebirth in the Pure Land of Ultimate Bliss but also a higher level and grade of rebirth. Aspiring practitioners should definitely not be content with rebirth in the lowest or middle level.

Aside from Huiyuan, Master Shandao's (善導; 613–681) says in his *Commentaries on the Sūtra on the Contemplation of Buddha Amitāyus*:

> ...in the true mind, one contemplates, observes, and yearns for Buddha Amitābha, as well as the direct retribution and the circumstantial retribution, as vividly as if they were right in front of one's own eyes.

> ...又真實心中，意業思想、觀察、憶念彼阿彌陀佛及依正二報，如現目前。[*Guan wuliangfo jing shu* 觀無量壽佛經疏: CBETA, T37, no. 1753, vol. 4, 272a9]

Obviously, how is it possible to achieve this without the power of meditative concentration? He further remarks:

> One should become mentally close and intimate [with the thought of Buddha], yearning for and recollecting [the Buddha] continuously, such is the uninterrupted practice."

> 心常親近，憶念不斷，名為無間行也。[*Guan wuliangfo jing shu* 觀無量壽佛經疏: CBETA, T37, no. 1753, vol. 4, 272a9]

In other words, all practices along this line unexceptionally require the power of meditative concentration. The author strongly advises all practitioners who seek rebirth in the Pure Land with a higher grade to complement their Pure Land cultivation by strengthening their proficiency in meditative concentration.

Note 6. Heavens of the desire realm: the mundane world is classified into three types of existence, or realms: the desire realm, the form realm, and the formless realm. The desire realm consists of the physical world and the six heavenly worlds (from the lowest heavenly plane, the Heaven of the Four Kings, up to the highest one, the Heaven of Comfort Gained Through Transformation of Other's Bliss). The desire realm is so named as all sentient beings born into it exhibit gender characteristics and possess sexual desire. The form realm is comprised of a total of eighteen heavens. Sentient beings that have attained the first to the fourth concentration, as well as the saints who have attained the third fruition of the Path to Liberation, reside in this realm. These sentient beings have a genderless physical form and do not conduct sexual behaviors. The formless realm is the dwelling of sentient beings that have attained the four formless absorptions. Inhabitants of the four heavens of the formless realm exist in purely mental state devoid of any physical attributes.

Note 7. Seeing the mountain as not being mountain, viewing the water as not being water: this verse describes the experience of Chan contemplation. Dwelling in a sense of doubt, a Chan practitioner contemplates so intensely and single-mindedly that he is oblivious to the surroundings. He sees and hears nothing despite healthy eyesight and hearing. For example, when he contemplates Chan as he walks home, he will pass by his own house without noticing it. When he contemplates Chan as he sits still, he will not see or hear anyone passing in front of him. He will only blink his eyes and start to see and hear again after he has come out of this state. It is at this point that he would realize that he had been in a state of "seeing the mountain as not being mountain," which is also referred to as the "dark barrel" or "mass of doubt."

Note 8. The specific vows of Buddhas: All Buddhas share the Four Vast Vows universally. The specific vows are made by Buddhas of past and present in the causal ground for sentient beings with respect to specific circumstances and conditions. As they are different from the Four Vast Vows and vary from Buddha to Buddha, they are called specific vows.

Note 9. Practitioners (行者): This practice method is primarily directed toward novice lay Buddhists, who are referred to as practitioners in this book.

Note 10. The *Sūtra on the Total Extinction of the Dharma* (法滅盡經; T12, no. 396) states:

> Men live shorter lives while women live longer to seventy, eighty, ninety, or even one hundred years of age…. At the time, there are bodhisattvas, pratyekabuddhas and arhats, who will be banished by gangs of demons from attending the assemblies of multitudes. [These noble disciples] of the Three Vehicles will come to the mountains, to a land of merits, where they delight in and are content with simple living and enjoy extended lifespans. Guarded

by celestial beings, [Bodhisattva] Moonlight will appear in the world, will meet these disciples, and together they will revive my Way for fifty-two years.

The *Śūraṅgama Sūtra* and the *Pratyutpannasamādhi Sūtra* (般舟三昧經; T13, no. 417 or 418) will first vanish. All sūtras in the twelve divisions will then soon follow. They will never reappear, and no text of them will remain. The kāṣāya robes of Buddhist monastics will naturally become white. My Dharma disappears from this world like an oil lamp, which blazes more brightly as it nears extinguishment. Then it just vanishes and will not be recounted and retold anymore. As such, in hundred millions of years thereafter, Bodhisattva Maitreya will become Buddha in this world, at a time of prosperity and peace, when all poisonous air have dispersed, and the five grains flourish with gentle and timely rain...

There are five translations of the *Sūtra on the Descent of Maitreya* (彌勒下生經): one by Dharmarakṣita (竺法護), two by Kumārajīva (鳩摩羅什), one by Yijing (義淨), and the fifth one by an anonymous translator. None of the first four versions explicitly accounts for the exact time when Bodhisattva Maitreya attains Buddhahood in this world; only the fifth version clearly states that, "Buddha Maitreya will be born and attain Buddhahood after about six billion years." However, in comparison to the previous four versions, a greater amount of the scriptural text is missing from this particular translation. Also, the name of its translator is unknown. Since the correctness of this translation is uncertain, the *Sūtra on the Total Extinction of the Dharma* was used as reference instead.

Note 11. The six sense objects: forms, sounds, odors, tastes, tactile objects, and mental phenomena.

Note 12. Meditative contemplation (思惟觀): Dwelling in a sense of doubt, a Chan practitioner contemplates single-mindedly on the doubt without using any language, sound, symbol, or image.

Note 13. Equal attention to both internal absorption and external discernment:

1. When a practitioner of Buddha-mindfulness engages in a conversation with another person without maintaining internal mental absorption, he will lose the thought of Buddha totally. Conversely, if he does not pay attention to the conversation (the external state) at all but focus entirely on the thought of Buddha (the internal state), he cannot comprehend what is being said. To understand the ongoing conversation and at the same time keep a clear and distinct thought of Buddha in mind, he must allocate equal attention to both internal absorption and external discernment.

2. A practitioner who has seen the Buddha-nature can see with the naked eye that his self-nature pervades all sense-fields—visual, auditory, olfactory, gustatory, tactile and mental. However, if he turns his attention to external states all the time, his power of meditative concentration will dissipate and in time he will gradually lose their ability to see the Buddha-nature. On the contrary, if he holds his mind totally inward, he will dwell in a state of mental absorption and cannot see the Buddha-

nature either.

If a practitioner who has seen the Buddha-nature can pay equal attention to both internal and external states, he will not regress from his attainment and can constantly see his self-nature. The sixth patriarch of the Chan school (Huineng) described this as "abiding in the self-nature in each and every thought," meaning that this is how one can spontaneously maintain and function within a state of meditative absorption. This, in fact, is only possible with the ability of either signless mindfulness of Buddha or the guarding of *huatou* in motion. Otherwise, one may have to nurture one's sacred attainment as a recluse.

3. If a practitioner who has attained the various levels of meditative absorptions (excluding those who have regressed from their attainment) can give equal attention to internal absorption and external discernment in daily life the way a practitioner of signless Buddha-mindfulness does, he can abide in the first concentration all the time and live a normal life like ordinary people without ever regressing from the first concentration.

Illustration of Buddha Prostration

Figure 1

Stand with your feet shoulder width apart. Relax and join your palms or cup them together in front of your chest. Close your eyes and balance your weight evenly on both feet.

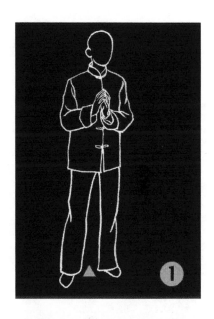

Figure 2:

Keep your palms joined as you slowly bend forward at the waist and move your weight forward.

Figure 3:

When you can no longer bend forward, start to bend your knees. Extend your right hand to touch the ground for support while shifting your weight forward.

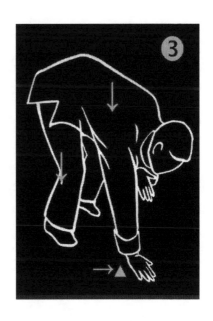

Figure 4:

Put your left hand down further forward and, using your arms for support, start to gently drop your knees until they touch the ground.

Figure 5:

Move your right
hand forward,
parallel with the
left hand, and let
the weight shift to
the back.

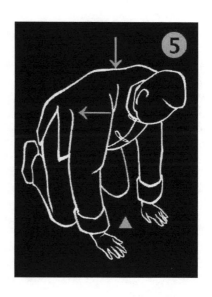

Figure 6:

Flatten your feet and rest your buttocks on your
calves. Bow down slowly until the forehead
touches the ground or mat. You can slightly
adjust your body to find a comfortable posture.

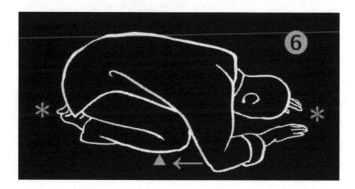

Figure 7:

Tuck your toes under and lift your body up slowly. Bring your weight onto your hands.

Figure 8:

Still leaning forward, lift your knees. Slowly step your hands closer to your body and begin to straighten your legs.

Figure 9:

Shift the weight onto the legs, push with both hands or just the right hand. Lift your body up as your hand(s) leave the ground.

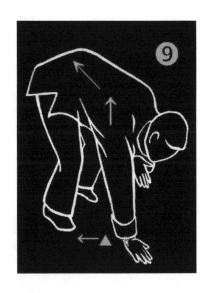

Figure 10:

With your weight securely on both legs, slowly straighten the torso to an upright position and bring the palms together.

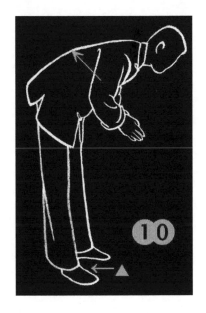

Figure 11:

Return to the starting posture with closed eyes, joined palms and legs parallel, shoulder width apart.

佛菩提二主要道次第概要表

The Cultivation Stages of the Two Paths within the Buddha Bodhi

二道並修，以外無別佛法

The joint cultivation of these two paths is the one and only way to attain Buddhahood

佛菩提道—大菩提 The Great Bodhi: Path to Buddhahood				解脫道— 二乘菩提 The Bodhi of the Two Lesser Vehicles: Path to Liberation
遠波羅蜜多 初信至十迴向 Distant Pāramitās ▶ From First Faith to Tenth Dedication	資糧位 Path of Accumulation	十信位修集信心 → 一劫乃至一萬劫 **Ten Faiths: Bodhisattvas accumulate faith in the Buddha Dharma. This will take one to ten thousand eons to accomplish.**	外門廣修六度萬行 Extensively practicing the six pāramitās before achieving awakening to the True Mind.	斷三縛結成初果解脫 Practitioners eliminate the three fetters to attain the first fruition of liberation.
		初住位修集布施功德（以財施為主）。 **First Abiding: Bodhisattvas collect virtues through charitable giving, primarily material goods.**		
		二住位修集持戒功德。 **Second Abiding: Bodhisattvas accumulate virtues through practicing the observance of precepts.**		
		三住位修集忍辱功德。 **Third Abiding: Bodhisattvas accumulate virtues through practicing forbearance.**		

155

Distant Pāra-mitās ▶ **From First Faith to Tenth Dedica-tion**	**Path of Accum-ulation**	四住位修集精進功德。 **Fourth Abiding: Bodhisattvas accumulate virtues through practicing diligence.**	**Extensively practicing the six pāramitās before achieving awakening to the True Mind.**	**Practitioners eliminate the three fetters to attain the first fruition of liberation.**
		五住位修集禪定功德。 **Fifth Abiding: Bodhisattvas accumulate virtues through practicing meditative absorption.**		
		六住位修集般若功德(熏習般若中觀及斷我見,加行位也)。 **Sixth Abiding: Bodhisattvas accumulate virtues through cultivating prajñā. They study and familiarize themselves with the principle of prajñā (the Middle Way) and eliminate the view of self during the Path of Preparation.**		
	見 道 位 **Path of Vision**	七住位明心——般若正觀現前,親證本來自性清淨涅槃。 **Seventh Abiding: Bodhisattvas awaken to the True Mind and gain direct comprehension of prajñā (the ultimate reality), thereupon realize directly and personally the nirvana with primordial, intrinsic and pure nature.**	內門廣修六度萬行 **Extensively practicing the six pāramitās after achieving awakening to the True Mind.**	薄貪瞋癡成二果解脫 **Practitioners attain the second fruition of liberation by reducing greed, aversion, and delusion.**
		八住位起於一切法現觀般若中道。漸除性障。 **Eighth Abiding: Starting from this stage, bodhisattvas gain direct comprehension of prajñā (the Middle Way) in all phenomena, and gradually eliminate the dispositional hindrances.**		
		十住位眼見佛性,世界如幻觀成就。 **Tenth Abiding: Bodhisattvas see the Buddha-nature with the physical eye and attain direct comprehension of the illusoriness of the world.**		

Distant Pāra-mitās ▶ From First Faith to Tenth Dedica-tion	**Path of Vision**	一至十行位，於廣行六度萬行中，依般若中道慧，現觀陰處界猶如陽焰。至第十行滿心位，陽焰觀成就。 First Practice to Tenth Practice: While extensively cultivating the six pāramitās, bodhisattvas rely on the wisdom of prajñā (the Middle Way) to directly comprehend that the five aggregates, twelve sense-fields, and eighteen elements are like mirages. Upon completing the Tenth Practice, they will have attained direct comprehension of the aggregates, sense-fields, and elements being like mirages. 一至十迴向位熏習一切種智；消除性障，唯留最後一分思惑不斷。第十迴向滿心位成就菩薩道如夢觀。 First Dedication to Tenth Dedication: Bodhisattvas study and familiarize themselves with the knowledge-of-all-aspects and eliminate dispositional hindrances, except the last bit of affliction eradicated through cultivation. Upon completing the Tenth Dedication, they will have attained direct comprehension of the bodhisattva path being like a dream.	Extensively practicing the six pāramitās after achieving awakening to the True Mind.	斷五下分結成三果解脫 Practitioners attain the third fruition of liberation by eliminating the five lower fetters.
近波羅蜜多　初地至七地	修道位	初地：第十迴向位滿心時，成就道種智一分（八識心王一一親證後，領受五法、三自性、七種第一義、七種性自性、二種無我法）復由勇發十無盡願，成通達位菩薩。復又永伏性障而不具斷，能證慧解脫而不取證，由大願故留惑潤生。此地主修法施波羅蜜多及百法明門。證「猶如鏡像」現觀，故滿初地心。 First Ground: Upon completing the Tenth Dedication, bodhisattvas will have realized a portion of the knowledge-of-the-aspects-of-paths, consisting of personal and direct realization of each		入地前的四加行令煩惱障現行悉斷，成四果解脫，留惑潤生。分段生死已斷，煩惱障習氣種子開始斷除，兼斷無始無明上煩惱。

Near Pāramitās ▶ From First Ground to Seventh Ground	**Path of Cultivation**	of the eight consciousnesses, which then enables them to perceive the five aspects of dharmas, the three natures, the seven facets of the ultimate truth, the seven intrinsic natures [of the tathāgatagarbha], and the two types of selflessness. They enter the Stage of Proficiency (First Ground) after bravely making the ten inexhaustible vows. Also, they have forever subdued the dispositional hindrances without eliminating them completely. While they can attain liberation from samsara through wisdom at this point, they purposely retain the last bit of afflictive hindrances to nourish future rebirths out of their great vows. The principal cultivation of the First Ground consists of the pāramitā of Dharma teaching as well as the Hundred Dharmas. The cultivation of the First Ground is completed when bodhisattvas attain direct comprehension of "[other-powered phenomena] being like images in a mirror."	Bodhisattvas undertake the four levels of intensified effort before entering the First Ground to eradicate the manifestation of all afflictive hindrances and attain the fourth fruition of liberation. However, the last bit of afflictive hindrances is purposely retained to nourish future rebirths. Bodhisattvas have put an end to delimited existence (*paricchedajarāmaraṇa*) and proceed to eliminate the habitual seeds of afflictive hindrances, as well as the higher afflictions of beginningless ignorance.
		二地：初地功德滿足以後，再成就道種智一分而入二地；主修戒波羅蜜多及一切種智。滿心位成就「猶如光影」現觀，戒行自然清淨。 Second Ground: Bodhisattvas enter the Second Ground when they have completed their cultivation of the First Ground and realized an additional portion of the knowledge-of-the-aspects-of-paths. Cultivation of this stage focuses on the pāramitā of precept observance and the knowledge-of-all-aspects. Upon completing the Second Ground, bodhisattvas will have attained direct comprehension of "[other-powered phenomena] being like light and shadows." Thereupon, they will be able to adhere to precepts in a way that is both pure and natural.	
		三地：二地滿心再證道種智一分，故入三地。此地主修忍波羅蜜多及四禪八定、四無量心、五神通。能成就俱解脫果而不取證，留惑潤生。滿心位成就「猶如谷響」現觀及無漏妙定意生身。 Third Ground: Bodhisattvas advance to the Third Ground after having realized an additional portion of the knowledge-of-the-aspects-of-paths upon completing the Second Ground. The principal cultivation of the Third Ground includes the pāramitā of forbearance, the four concentrations and the four formless absorptions, the four	

boundless minds, as well as the five supernatural powers. While bodhisattvas on the Third Ground can realize the fruition of twofold liberation, they deliberately choose not to; instead, they purposely retain the last bit of afflictive hindrances to nourish future rebirths. Upon completing the Third Ground, bodhisattvas will have attained direct comprehension of "[other-powered phenomena] being like echoes in a valley" and achieved the "mind-made body attained through the taintless and wondrous samādhi."

Near Pāramitās

▶

From First Ground to Seventh Ground

Path of Cultivation

四地：由三地再證道種智一分故入四地。主修精進波羅蜜多，於此土及他方世界廣度有緣，無有疲倦。進修一切種智，滿心位成就「如水中月」現觀。

Fourth Ground: Bodhisattvas advance to the Fourth Ground after having realized an additional portion of the knowledge-of-the-aspects-of-paths on the Third Ground. The principal cultivation of this stage is the pāramitā of diligence, for which bodhisattvas extensively and tirelessly teach and guide sentient beings who have karmic connections with them in this and other worlds. They will also continue their cultivation of the knowledge-of-all-aspects. Upon completing the Third Ground, bodhisattvas will have attained direct comprehension of "[other-powered phenomena] being like the moon reflected in the water."

五地：由四地再證道種智一分故入五地。主修禪定波羅蜜多及一切種智，斷除下乘涅槃貪。滿心位成就「變化所成」現觀。

Fifth Ground: Bodhisattvas advance to the Fifth Ground after having realized an additional portion of the knowledge-of-the-aspects-of-paths on the Fourth Ground. The pāramitā of meditative absorption and the knowledge-of-all-aspects constitute the principal cultivation of the Fifth Ground. Bodhisattvas will also eliminate their desire for the nirvana attained in the lesser vehicles. Upon completing the Fifth Ground, they will have attained direct comprehension of "[other-powered phenomena] being like the effects of conjuring."

Near Pāramitās ▶ From First Ground to Seventh Ground	**Path of Cultivation**	六地：由五地再證道種智一分故入六地。此地主修般若波羅蜜多--依道種智現觀十二因緣一一有支及意生身化身，皆自心真如變化所現，「似有非有」，成就細相觀，不由加行而自然證得滅盡定，成俱解脫大乘無學。 Sixth Ground: Bodhisattvas advance to the Sixth Ground after having realized an additional portion of the knowledge-of-the-aspects-of-paths on the Fifth Ground. The principal cultivation of the Sixth Ground is the pāramitā of prajñā: relying on the knowledge-of-the-aspects-of-paths they have acquired, bodhisattvas directly comprehend that each of the twelve links of dependent arising as well as the mind-made emanation bodies are all transformations of one's mind of True Suchness, and therefore are "seemingly but not truly existent." They accomplish the contemplation of the subtle characteristics of all phenomena and acquire the ability to spontaneously realize the meditative absorption of cessation without any added effort. Thereupon, they become Mahāyāna adepts (aśaikṣa) of twofold liberation.	
		七地：由六地「似有非有」現觀，再證道種智一分故入七地。此地主修一切種智及方便波羅蜜多，由重觀十二有支一一支中之流轉門及還滅門一切細相，成就方便善巧，念念隨入滅盡定。滿心位證得「如犍闥婆城」現觀。 Seventh Ground: After gaining direct comprehension that [other-powered phenomena] are "seemingly but not truly existent" on the Sixth Ground, bodhisattvas attain an additional portion of the knowledge-of-the-aspects-of-paths and advance to the Seventh Ground. The cultivation of the Seventh Ground focuses on continued learning of the knowledge-of-all-aspects and the pāramitā of skillful means. Additionally, bodhisattvas contemplate again all the subtle characteristics of each of the twelve factors of dependent arising from the perspectives of transmigration and the extinction of transmigration, whereby they achieve mastery of skillful means and the ability to enter the meditative absorption of cessation in a single thought. Upon completing the Seventh Ground, bodhisattvas will have attained direct comprehension of "[other-powered phenomena] being as illusory as a gandharva's city."	七地滿心斷除故意保留之最後一分思惑時，煩惱障所攝色、受、想三陰有漏習氣種子同時斷盡。 Upon completing the Seventh Ground, bodhisattvas will have eliminated the last bit of "affliction eradicated through cultivation" that has been purposely retained. They will also have thoroughly eliminated all tainted

				habitual seeds of afflictive hindrances associated with the aggregates of form, sensation, and perception.
大波羅蜜多 Great Pāramitās ▶ From Eighth Ground to Virtual Enlightenment	八地至等覺	Path of Cultivation	八地：由七地極細相觀成就故再證道種智一分而入八地。此地主修一切種智及願波羅蜜多。至滿心位純無相觀任運恆起，故於相土自在，滿心位復證「如實覺知諸法相意生身」故。 Eighth Ground: Having attained the contemplation of the extremely subtle characteristics at the Seventh Ground, bodhisattvas realize an additional portion of the knowledge-of-the-aspects-of-paths and advance to the Eighth Ground. The principal cultivation of the Eighth Ground concentrates on the continued learning of the knowledge-of-all-aspects and the pāramitā of vows. Upon completing the Eighth Ground, bodhisattvas will be able to spontaneously bring forth the contemplation of signlessness at all times and hence can manipulate physical objects or mental images at will. Also, they will have realized "the mind-made body attained through correct realization of dharma characteristics." 九地：由八地再證道種智一分故入九地。主修力波羅蜜多及一切種智，成就四無礙，滿心位證得「種類俱生無行作意生身」。 Ninth Ground: Bodhisattvas advance to the Ninth Ground after having realized an additional portion of the knowledge-of-the-aspects-of-paths on the Eighth Ground. The principal cultivation of the Ninth Ground consists of the pāramitā of strength as well as continued learning of the knowledge-of-all-aspects. Upon completing the Ninth Ground, bodhisattvas will have mastered the four unhindered knowledges and realized "the mind-made body attained without added effort and in accordance with the classes of beings to be delivered."	煩惱障所攝行、識二陰無漏習氣種子任運漸斷，所知障所攝上煩惱任運漸斷。 Bodhisattvas gradually and spontaneously eliminate the taintless habitual seeds of afflictive hindrances associated with the aggregates of formation and consciousness, as well as the higher afflictions of cognitive hindrances.

Great Pāra-mitās ▶ From Eighth Ground to Virtual Enlight-enment	**Path of Culti-vation**	十地：由九地再證道種智一分故入此地。此地主修一切種智--智波羅蜜多。滿心位起大法智雲，及現起大法智雲所含藏種種功德，成受職菩薩。 Tenth Ground: Bodhisattvas advance to the Tenth Ground after having realized an additional portion of the knowledge-of-the-aspects-of-paths on the Ninth Ground. The principal cultivation of the Tenth Ground is the knowledge-of-all-aspects, namely, the pāramitā of omniscience. Upon completing the Tenth Ground, bodhisattvas will be able to generate the cloud of great Dharma wisdom and manifest the various meritorious qualities contained therein. They will also become a "designated bodhisattva." 等覺：由十地道種智成就故入此地。此地應修一切種智，圓滿等覺地無生法忍，於百劫中修集極廣大福德，以之圓滿三十二大人相及無量隨形好。 Virtual Enlightenment: After having realized the portion of the knowledge-of-the-aspects-of-paths cultivated on the Tenth Ground, bodhisattvas advance to the stage of Virtual Enlightenment. At this stage, they cultivate the knowledge-of-all-aspects and perfectly realize the acquiescence to the non-arising of dharmas pertaining to this stage. They will also perfect the thirty-two majestic physical features and innumerable associated good marks unique to Buddha by cultivating and accumulating enormous amount of virtues over a hundred eons.	Bodhisattvas gradually and spontaneously eliminate the taintless habitual seeds of afflictive hindrances associated with the aggregates of formation and consciousness, as well as the higher afflictions of cognitive hindrances.
圓滿波羅蜜多	究竟位	妙覺：示現受生人間，已斷盡煩惱障一切習氣種子，並斷盡所知障一切隨眠，永斷變易生死無明，成就大般涅槃，四智圓明。人間捨壽後，報身常住色究竟天利樂十方地上菩薩；以諸化身利樂有情，永無盡期，成就究竟佛道。 Sublime Enlightenment: Bodhisattvas have thoroughly eliminated all habitual seeds of afflictive hindrances and all latent cognitive hindrances, as well as permanently eradicated the ignorance that leads to transformational existence. They will manifest birth in the human world, realize the great nirvana, and perfect the	斷盡變易生死, 成就大般涅槃。

Perfect Pāra-mitās	Path of Ultimate Realization	four kinds of wisdom of Buddha. After displaying physical death in the human world, their reward-bodies will permanently reside in the highest heaven of the form-realm to continue to teach and guide bodhisattvas on or above the First Ground coming from all worlds. Having accomplished the ultimate fruition of Buddhahood, they will generate numerous emanation bodies to perpetually teach and guide sentient beings.	Bodhisattvas bring transfor-mational existence (*parinamikijarā marana*) to a complete end and attain the great nirvana.

圓 滿 成 就 究 竟 佛 果

Perfect Ultimate Fruition of Buddhahood

Respectfully composed by Buddhist disciple Xiao Pingshi. (Feb. 2012)

Cultivation Centers of the True Enlightenment Practitioners Association

Taipei True Enlightenment Lecture Hall
9F, No. 277, Sec. 3, Chengde Rd., Taipei 103, Taiwan, R.O.C.
Tel.: +886-2-2595-7295
(Ext. 10 & 11 for 9F; 15 & 16 for 10F; 18 & 19 for 5F; and 14 for the bookstore on 10F.)
Daxi True Enlightenment Patriarch Hall
No. 5-6, Kengdi, Ln. 650, Xinyi Rd., Daxi Township, Taoyuan County 335, Taiwan, R.O.C.
Tel.: +886-3-388-6110
Taoyuan True Enlightenment Lecture Hall
10F, No. 286 & 288, Jieshou Rd., Taoyuan 330, Taiwan, R.O.C.
Tel.: +886-3-374-9363
Hsinchu True Enlightenment Lecture Hall
2F-1, No. 55, Dongguang Rd., Hsinchu 300, Taiwan, R.O.C.
Tel.: +886-3-572-4297
Taichung True Enlightenment Lecture Hall
13F-4, No. 666, Sec. 2, Wuquan W. Rd., Nantun Dist., Taichung 408, Taiwan, R.O.C.
Tel.: +886-4-2381-6090
Jiayi True Enlightenment Lecture Hall
8F-1, No. 288, Youai Rd., Jiayi 600, Taiwan, R.O.C.
Tel.: +886-5-231-8228
Tainan True Enlightenment Lecture Hall
4F, No. 15, Sec. 4, Ximen Rd., Tainan 700, Taiwan, R.O.C.
Tel.: +886-6-282-0541
Kaohsiung True Enlightenment Lecture Hall
5F, No. 45, Zhongzheng 3rd Rd., Kaohsiung 800, Taiwan, R.O.C.
Tel.: +886-7-223-4248
Los Angeles True Enlightenment Lecture Hall
825 S. Lemon Ave, Diamond Bar, CA 91789, U.S.A.
Tel.: +1-909-595-5222   Cell: +1-626-454-0607
Hong Kong True Enlightenment Lecture Hall
Unit E1, 27th Floor, TG Place, 10 Shing Yip Street, Kwun Tong, Kowloon, Hong Kong
Tel: +852-2326-2231

Website of the True Enlightenment Practitioners Association:
http://www.enlighten.org.tw
Website of the True Wisdom Publishing Co.:
http://books.enlighten.org.tw

Readers may download free publications of the Association from the above website.